How to Sing

Practical Exercises for Smooth Singing

(A Complete Guide to Creating Stronger Performances)

Michael Arwood

Published By **Jordan Levy**

Michael Arwood

How to Sing: Practical Exercises for Smooth Singing (A Complete Guide to Creating Stronger Performances)

ISBN   978-1-998038-98-5

No part of this guidebook shall be reproduced in any form without permission in writing from the publisher except in the case of brief quotations embodied in critical articles or reviews.

Legal & Disclaimer

The information contained in this book is not designed to replace or take the place of any form of medicine or professional medical advice. The information in this book has been provided for educational & entertainment purposes only.

The information contained in this book has been compiled from sources deemed reliable, and it is accurate to the best of the Author's knowledge; however, the Author cannot guarantee its accuracy and validity and cannot be held liable for any errors or omissions. Changes are periodically made to this book. You must consult your doctor or get professional medical advice before using any of the suggested remedies, techniques, or information in this book.

Table Of Contents

Chapter 1: Getting Started and What To Expect

Singing a hundred and one

You will learn how to put together your hobby earlier than you start exercising. For example you may want to set a time for exercise that doesn't interfere together along with your ingesting time desk. You wouldn't need to sing on a complete stomach of meals due to the fact it may cause a lazy overall performance. I inspire you to have your meal about an hour or a half of hour before you start. That manner your meals is digested and out of the manner and not actually sitting to your belly geared up to be processed. You will learn how to do matters singers do ordinary to put together themselves for growing a track engagements or performances. It doesn't matter number if you are self taught or reading with a expert vocal trainer. You can be given the 'the way to's' needed to put together you for your vocal endeavors.

This ebook will help you with becoming a greater assured singer. It isn't designed to teach you everything about making a song. Yet you may gain sensible information inside the capacity to demonstrate real approach, shape and sound extremely good. .

Your Image of You.

What this segment of the e-book in brief specializes in is more of a highbrow thing of approaches you can need to go through in thoughts viewing your voice, and the sounds it makes, for the most effective very last results. What do you observed you sound like? I'm positive we've all had a person touch upon the manner they assume our voice sounds to them. Well, if so, then we also can have developed a concept of methods we recognize our voice primarily based at the accolades of others and/or the terrible remarks. Either way I'm here to share with you a completely particular point of method. Understand this: out of the billions upon billions of beings born upon this beautiful earth, you are uniquely and splendidly made. Your voice is the best one you can ever acquire. Accept it and discover it irresistible. The sounds you're making are yours and that they've been made to suit into the rest of the lovely sounds of this universe.

Chapter 2: Singing with Proper Body Alignment

Breathing

Let's speak approximately breath in advance than we get into posture. Breath is what gives us earthly beings our existence pressure. Okay, I'm sure every body agree that we want breath to live, correct? Singing requires us to apply proper breathing. If we use breath within the proper manner, we're able to sing a music without a trouble. If we use it incorrectly, we can battle through even a easy phrase in a track. So pretty obviously, we ought to recognition at the energy of breath that is being pulled upon at the equal time as we talk and sing. Breath is a pal to the vocalist. We need to use as a exceptional deal breath as desired whilst we are creating a music. As a vocal teach it is my mission to train students to breathe nicely while singing. For example, you wouldn't want to be bending over or slouched over while you are trying to sing a tune, because you may block the airway from successfully projecting your sound great. Instead, you will want to be recognition up right now simply so the breath can float out easily. Knowing whilst to take a breath is also crucial to the singer due to the truth it is able to make or destroy how properly you sound on the same time as making a music your tune. You never need to sound like you are walking out of breath in the center of a tune or word. Nor should you want to sound "winded", as despite the fact that you're going to crumble in advance than finishing the phrase. The sound incredible, irrespective of how easy or loud, need to be full and virtually controlled. A wonderful exercise is to take a breath at some point of every four-eight counts or beats consistent with measure of the tune. I will provide an example under of a super vocal workout I use to help students studies wherein to take their breaths inside the route of a music.

Exercise 1:

Take the music "Mary Had A Little Lamb". Sing it exactly the way you are analyzing it to complete this exercise. Inhale a deep breath and sing out multi feature breath for four region take a look at beats (counts)...

Sing:

Ma ry Had A...

Do that every one in one breath.

Then take some one-of-a-kind breath and sing:

Lit tle Lamb

Do that each one in a unmarried breath

Inhale a few different breath and sing:

Lit tle lamb

Do that every one in a unmarried breath

 Inhale some different breath and sing:

Inhale all over again and entire the word:

Lit tle lamb

This workout is completed on a 4 depend the use of 4/4 time signature this means that that 4 area be aware beats in step with degree.

The reason of this exercising is to expose you the manner to practice taking in breaths after each quick phrase. A phrase is normally one to 2 measures lengthy. Practice this over and over till it turns into 2d nature. You can begin first by using using manner of just clapping at a steady pace. As you're clapping, begin to recall from one to 4, then circulate lower returned to 1 and repeat the trouble all over again. Next, begin creating a tune the primary line. Then keep the rest of the workout on the same pace. This manner you'll experience the phrases synchronize with the beat. This exercise allows to show you in which to take proper breaths at the give up of every word.

Exercise 2:

You will use the equal tune "Mary Had A Little Lamb" for this workout. Sing the tune exactly the manner it's miles written. Inhale a deep breath and sing out for eight beats (counts)...This will let you train your self on a way to inhale each eight beats or counts constant with word.

Sing:

Ma ry had A... Lit tle Lamb

Do that each one in a unmarried breath.

Then take every one of a kind breath and sing:

Lit tle lamb... Lit tle Lamb

This exercise is performed on an eight remember which incorporates eight location be aware beats. That ismeasures with 4 beats in every.

You have just sung, Mary Had A Little Lamb (on an eight do not forget). That need to be executed multi function breath. Practice this 4-8 times.

You need to continually recollect to depend upon the breath to maintain you thru a phrase. Taking one breath to sing a full eight bar phase without a doubt is the goal! Make smart breath alternatives. If you sense yourself out of breath take every other one at that precise point. Follow the ones commands and you will become accurate at taking breaths in amongst phrases correctly.

A couple of steps to consider on the same time as focusing at the breath:

1. Awareness of your body equals mindfulness of breath. Duration and period equals how extended your inhalation is and how prolonged your exhalation may be. You can adjust and have a look at these items through recognition and focusing on the breath as you are breathing in and out.

2. Practice growing your volume of breath consumption. You can do this thru measuring how an lousy lot air it takes to top off and increase your lungs even as you're inhaling. For example, you'll inhale and start counting alongside to your head or hands. This will diploma how lengthy it takes to top off your lungs with air. It is fine to do that even as fame. The purpose is on the manner to inhale as a bargain as 12-16 counts.

Exercise 3:

1.Stand right away, with toes shoulder width apart. Place your arms on your belly. Take in a breath. Begin to gauge the depth of the breath collectively along with your arms on your stomach. Watch how your arms will pass internal and out as you inhale and exhale. As you're monitoring the air stepping into and out, word how it's also touring all within the course of your frame. This breathing technique want to reason a chilled sensation. Each time you try this, you will look at increasingly the manner to modify the breath. You will learn how to maintain longer notes and breath with a good deal a great deal less try.

2.Inhale through the nose to create an opening and growth of the chest; exhale through the mouth to deflate and drop the chest. Also, as you are doing this you will be preserving a regular rely or beat. You will now not need to place hobby at the depend variety. Stay focused at the breath and allow the depend come sincerely similar to the beat of your coronary coronary heart.

3.Focus on the length of breath. Duration offers with the period of time you are able to hold your breath in addition to the quantity. You need to increase the pressure. This allows you to build up your respiration great. Your strain growth seems some thing like whilst you're blowing air right right into a balloon and the quantity of air forces it to growth outward. You experience whilst air is going into your lungs down past your chest into the stomach location elevating up the diaphragm. Envision this taking place as you are reading a way to do it.

Posture

This is enormously vital for the singer. Your sound splendid will rely on how properly you are the usage of posture to assist your notes and breath. You don't need to be slouched over or bent within the incorrect position while you are trying to sing because of the reality the sound can be stricken by it. You moreover don't need to dam your sound from popping out of your mouth sincerely. Putting pressure inside the incorrect areas of your frame will intervene with sound exceptional sooner or later of making a song. Stand immediately up collectively along with your knees slightly bent just so they aren't in a locked function. Then take a deep breath and sing out. You need your neck to be right away and your head going through beforehand. Your once more want to additionally be right away, no longer slouched inward. You do not need your head to be returned and face in the direction of the ceiling because of the reality you could not be able to successfully manipulate your respiratory that manner. The tremendous sound first rate will encompass correct posture.

The Head Voice

What does it virtually propose while people say 'sing out of your head voice' ? This is truely regarding the location of the sound resonating off of your vocal chords. It will experience similar to the sound is coming from the top of your head due to the truth you could sense a robust vibration to your better frame and in particular to your head even as the notes are being sung. It additionally refers to your vocal range and the place it resonates from at the same time as you are making a song the excessive notes. It's crucial to realize that the top voice is more potent than the falsetto voice. It is your vocal chords doing most of the artwork, not surely your head. But whilst you sing and are hitting your excessive notes, it feels similar to the sound or vibration is to your head. That is likewise due to the fact the sound is traveling in an upward position in the direction of the pinnacle of your mouth hole space. So, each time you pay interest a person say, sing from your "head voice" you may recognize what that means.

An instance of the top voice is Lizzo's "Truth Hurts". In the hole line she says " Why men notable…" It appears like a belt sensation and the position is ahead within the the the the the front of the mouth.

It's now not to be burdened in conjunction with your falsetto. Although falsetto notes are without a doubt high they're additionally very breathy and airy. Plus your falsetto may be felt in both your chest vicinity in addition to the pinnacle.

Chapter 3: Singing from the Diaphragm

Vibration and Tones

There is a distinction a number of the chest and the diaphragm? Singing from the diaphragm is even as the breath is coming from the lowest of the belly area. It is in which you experience maximum comfortable and cushty speakme from. This is commonly the lower take a look at in of the voice. The tone and textures are an awful lot deeper, fuller and richer. You will surely experience the vibration tones on your chest location while you sing notes however, the breath placement is inside the bottom of the diaphragm. You might also have the entire vocal cords vibrating and the diaphragm engaged while creating a tune and speaking.

The chest wall is where the ribs are positioned among distinct vital body factors. The muscle corporations a few of the ribs and determination are what increases the chest and lowers it. The breath flows downward into that area to permit the air to circulate and convey once more up exceptional or horrible sound, in quantity, relying for your body posture.

Breathe into your mouth and supply the air downward to the chest . Notice how your shoulders begin to boom up and outward. When that takes placeyou are the use of your chest in region of your diaphragm.

This is now and again called a shallow breath as it isn't in reality as sturdy due to the reality the diaphragm breath. You can get a few short and brilliant sounds while respiratory out of your chest however it isn't recommended for the motive that fullest and most supported sounds may be coming from taking in a large quantity of air and sending it right right down to your stomach- diaphragm area. This lets in the first-class of sound to be supported for the furthest distance and sound.

There is a few thing I name the Buddha Belly breath technique. I use it to show college students the way to sing absolutely while hitting the excessive notes in heaps tons less than half of-hour of normal practice. It's quite clean to do. Here is what you will do…

1.Stand tall along with your once more immediately however do now not lock your knees as this may limit the air because of the fact you're surely preserving in anxiety even as any a part of your body is "locked". You need to sense the natural go together with the float of air during your entire whole body.

2.Next, inhale a deep breath and slowly permit it out. Do that 3 times to get warmed up.

3.To hold, take a 'Buddha Belly Breath' thru breathing in in as lots air you may with out straining your rib cage. Allow your belly to poke out as a long way as it could move. Imagine the 'Buddha' at the identical time as you are doing this.

4. Hold that for 2 counts then launch it on the sound of : Ahhhh Mmmm

5. Be certain to open and close to your mouth three instances until you now not have any air left. Feel the air leaving your frame as your stomach deflates backpedal. Relax your shoulders into it.

6. Now that your lungs are empty, begin all over again with the aid of taking in a deep breath. Repeat this step approximately nine times for wonderful effects.

Vocal Techniques

In this ebook I reputation on what I get hold of as true with the maximum essential strategies are for buying any amateur commenced out inside the right manner. That being stated, there are such a whole lot of particular and massive techniques to creating a track effectively. However allow's slim it down to three number one but important ones. The first goes to be hitting the excessive notes well. We use pressure, force and breath to attain as much as a excessive take a look at. We in no manner want to stress at the same time as doing so and this is why posture and proper breathing is taught up the the front. When you're making a song songs there are terms and dynamic adjustments all at some stage in the track. So we address one word at a time using the proper dynamics and breathing. Your method to a word is top. The beginning of the phrase, the center of the phrase and the completing of the phrase determines the overall phrase. When you begin the phrase you need to generally take a deep breath to begin. You want to be in the maximum comfortable kingdom of thoughts as feasible. You also can enjoy aggravating at the equal time as making a track within the front of a crowd and if that takes area hold in mind to respire and lighten up. You might also moreover use critical stress to provide the sound a few more extent. Remember the breathing method we mentioned in advance. Deep breath in and send it right all the way down to your diaphragm. Then slowly launch it on an exhale at the same time as allowing the tone to overlay the breath. While inside the center of the phrase, loosen up into the breath as you are making a song the terms. This prevents you from on foot out of breath and collapsing the study. Do now not strain the breath out even as growing a tune the word. Allow the sound to go with the float out and you may experience the breath and vibration as you keep and whole the word correctly. So, combine your inhale with the start of the word and release the terms over the tones.. The breath facilitates to preserve notes. This is some thing that need to be practiced regularly. Your nice strategies will most effective embody workout. You will see improvement and a change in your sound as you start to practice those and the opposite techniques.

Pitch and Diction

When you pay attention someone speakme about pitch in making a tune you automatically apprehend they may be regarding the immoderate and espresso frequencies of the vocal range. A person's voice tiers everywhere from a soprano, mezzo-soprano, alto, tenor, baritone on proper all the manner down to a bass. For instance, If you have a voice that is able to sing more excessive notes you'll maximum possibly be considered to have a soprano vocal range. . In the middle of the vocal tiers is the alto. At the lowest of the vocal variety is the tenor. And on the very low backside is the bass or baritone vocal range.

The vocal variety is some thing that may be informed to increase higher and lower. If you want to increase your vocal variety you want to practice doing so. Although you have been born together together with your precise sound, with schooling you may normally decorate it. Again, you need to train the voice if you need it to broaden. Musical scales are a superb way to help you in schooling the voice for higher pitch.

Diction found with the pitch is surprisingly important for a singer. Diction specializes within the manner the terms sound coming out of the mouth. This is important with growing a music because of the fact the manner you pronounce the phrase determines how properly it will sound to the ears of the listener. Therefore , you want your phrase to be understood while you're making a song. We will do a little examples with diction to get a richer records.

Take the ones vowels and say them slowly exactly as they will be written.

1. Say the A - Ah ay: Ah sound first and then upload the ay sound after.

2. Say the E - Eh ee: Eh sound first then upload the ee sound very last.

3. Say the I - Ee aye: Ee sound first then upload the aye sound very last

4. Say the O - Oh oo: Oh sound first then add the oo sound ultimate.

5. Say the U - Oo uh: Oo sound first then upload the uh sound final.

First exercise announcing every person vowel and enunciate with clean diction. Say the vowel with identical emphasis on each syllable (i.E Ah-ay). Do that severa instances to get your mouth and vocal chords all warmed up. Do now not cut up the sound.You need to preserve the be conscious count number range range for approximately four beats after which bypass on to the subsequent vowel until you have said all of them.

Second step is to duplicate the preceding steps with a sixty second loosen up duration in amongst. Then flow into at once to the following vowel and do the same for 6 - 9 instances until you have got accomplished all of them.

Lastly, make certain to start off in a very comfortable state. Resonate in your backside chest voice to start. This is the lowest pitch your voice is able to do effortlessly. Your vocal capability isn't always to be in comparison with every one-of-a-kind character. Your variety can be based totally to your private genetic make up and that is what determines how excessive or low your voice is going.

You will discover your variety with out difficulty through gambling notes on both a piano, keyboard or guitar. Go to any piano and find Middle C. This is likewise called C4 (the 4th C positioned at the keyboard). It is in the center 1/2 of most keyboards. Sit on the piano. Play the attention after which try to sing alongside to wholesome the sound you pay interest. If you're able to sing it really then your vocal variety sits somewhere internal that check in of the piano/ keyboard. If you find out your self struggling to sing the word then you definately genuinely definately want to transport on to the following be conscious at the keyboard. Sing until you hit the very notable phrase with out straining and then mark that spot.

A latest exercising for ladies's voices is to begin at Middle C on the keyboard and cross up closer to the right of the keyboard. A sizable workout for a man's voice is to begin at C4 and paintings down the dimensions within the direction of the left of Middle C. The higher notes are in the course of the right of Middle C and the lower notes are in the course of the left of Middle C. Either manner, to locate your correct range you can want to move up and down the dimensions. The purpose is to ensure no longer to damage your vocal cords with the useful resource of straining them in any other case you could do important harm. If you're cracking at the same time as creating a track a observe most probable you are not capable of sing that phrase and it's miles out of your vocal variety.

Look on the picture underneath. To assist you locate Middle C you may rely down 5 white keys beginning from the left of this photograph. It is the 5th white key some of the 3 black keys and the to white keys. .

Chapter 4: Keeping the Beat

Rhythm is Key

The rhythm is the beat, tempo and motion pattern your song will journey on the equal time as you sing. It isn't unusual to make up rhythm patterns the usage of 4 beats consistent with degree or 3 beats according to degree. Rhythm is in all kinds of tune. Your coronary coronary heart beats to a rhythm. Rhythm flows in some unspecified time in the future of the tune; It drives the existence pressure of the tune through vibration and tones. In music, rhythm enables create the natural cycle and changes which you pay attention at some stage in the music.

This exercising will awareness on rhythm through track. When you're making a music you have to go with the flow to and fro, or faucet your toes, or snap your fingers, or clap your hands. Whichever you choose out will sincerely assist to get a regular rhythm flowing before you start to start making a song along.

Start with the resource of tapping your toes at a regular tempo. Count out loud from 1-4. Repeat that count some times to get a ordinary tempo. Start creating a music the terms to "Row Row Row Your Boat". Don't prevent the rhythm and motion absolutely replace the numbers with the phrases. Sing that over and over a few instances until it starts offevolved offevolved to revel in comfortable. Play spherical with the pace of your rhythm at the same time as you sing the phrases. Get into the exercise of converting your tempo. You can select any song you want and do this exercise as part of your every day vocal heat up.

The Importance of Practice

They say practice makes satisfactory. Not precisely. It is true that remarkable exercising makes development. In order to have a look at any new potential and do it effectively you want to create and determine to training it. There isn't any manner round exercise at the same time as you are getting to know the way to sing and bring a first-rate tone. Practice will help you train and supply a lift for your vocal chords just like a person who practices how to make stronger and tone his body muscle tissues.

Dedicate yourself to a exercising ordinary and you may no longer be upset because of the truth your voice will provide you with once more what you placed into it. It permits you properly use your voice on the equal time as creating a tune and to keep away from injuries in the approach. You begin to study your voice's strengths , weaknesses, on the facet of growing your range. It is within the exercise in which you may research and discover the particular tones and textures of your voice! Below is a every day exercising guide you can begin using now. And don't forget about, every example stated within the previous chapters can and need to be introduced as a part of your exercising everyday.

This step by step exercise manual is designed to provide a every day vocal lesson warm up for proper body alignment and tone.

Total Body Warm Up

Step 1. Stretch your fingers up within the air and Inhale. Extend your stomach out on the identical time as inhaling.

Step 2. Next as you're exhaling, bend over all the way all the manner all the way down to the floor as some distance as you could skip with out harming your again. If you feel tightness in the returned or lower legs prevent at that factor and go back once more up. Touch your toes if viable. Don't stress. Relax. Come lower lower returned up. While you're coming decrease again up, inhale a few distinctive deep breath. Stretch your fingers up inside the air again and repeat the previous step.

Step three. Repeat nine instances slowly

Total Body warmth up with sound

Step 1. Inhale a deep breath after which say the word HOO-ooo-ooo as you are exhaling all of the air out of your lungs. Listen to the body and the sound.

Step 2. Inhale a deep breath and then say the word "Nayyyyyyyy" as you are exhaling all of the air from your lungs. Don't overlook about to take note of the frame and sound.

Step 3. Do a few exceptional set of 9. You want to sense really snug.

Voice heat up

Step 1. Inhale a deep breath via your mouth and at the exhale say: hummm-ummmm Start at the low register of your voice and climb up the size to the pinnacle of the octave. Do this while preserving your mouth closed.

Step 2. After all of the air is about loose, take in a few different breath (If you're capable of sing to the subsequent octave maintain up to the following octave. If not, please circulate again to the start) and begin another time. Repeat nine instances.

The purpose is to educate your voice to transport from one octave to the second after which the 1/three resultseasily.

Volume and dynamics

Step 1. You can do that exercising in different procedures to add range and dynamics. Begin on a soft tone the number one time thru then go from smooth to medium.

Step 2. Go from loud to very loud. Make positive to mission your sound outward. Say those open vowels the usage of a big open mouth :

Naaaaaaa (begin smooth -then go up in amount)

Neeee (start easy -then skip up in quantity)

Niiiiiiiiii (begin smooth -then float up in extent)

Nooooooo (start easy -then cross up in quantity)

Nuuuuuuu (begin smooth -then skip up in volume)

3.Rhythm

Good rhythm is an important part of a first-rate voice. Simply placed, you need to sound clean, no longer uneven. One of the super strategies to sound smooth is with the aid of extending your vowel sounds and sliding your phrases collectively. For instance, whilst you are saying bus save you, it ought to sound extra like busstop.

Note: To boom rhythm, waft your arm at some point of your body in a smooth way as you speak. Focus on connecting your speakme with the drift of the movement. Notice how your vowel sounds expand absolutely; additionally observe the general, rich sound you're making as you remember connecting.

4.Pacing (Breath Control)

Pacing is vital to characteristic intensity and duration to your voice. You have to speak in short sentences — now not prolonged, complex sentences. When you talk in lengthy complicated sentences, you commonly will be inclined to cram greater terms into one breath.

Note: When you compress your sounds, you're turning into more phrases proper proper into a breath and sucking out the tone and color of your voice. Remember, tempo yourself. Speak in brief sentences supported through small breath. Examples of short breath-sentences songs are There Is a King in You through Donald Lawrence & I Won't Go Back with the resource of William McDowell to call some.

Vocal Health Tips

Whether you are an aspiring singer, you already sing professionally otherwise you sing in the bathe for amusing, searching after your voice ought to be a top priority. Here I'm going to percentage with you few pointers that I've given to many one in every of a kind college college students and characteristic worked for them.

1.Quality Sleep

Lack of sleep is an enemy of the voice and singers have to sleep properly to sing well. Every night time, our body requires a fantastic quantity of great rest to recharge and repair. When your body is fatigued, your voice is simply too. A whole 8 hours of slumber the night time time before a vocal trendy performance will help best voice extraordinary.

2.Good Ventilation

Whatever you're breathing in from your environment affects your voice and throat. On the forestall of the scale, cigarette smoking and smoke tool will salary struggle to your vocal twine but even a few aspect as seemingly innocent as a centrally heated room with low humidity can motive your throat to dehydrate and suffer as impact.

3.Hydration (Keep Well Water)

Whether it's a tap water or mineral, keeping your device properly hydrated with eight glasses of although water a day is as wholesome on your voice as it is to your body. Avoid ice water purpose that shape of cold is an unpleasant wonder to the vocal cords and they'll tighten up in a right away.

4.Wear A Scarf

Sudden exchange in temperature can play havoc at the side of your voice. If you are going from the warmth to an air-conditioned room or vice versa, your voice will experience it. Aside wearing a headband, in case you're cold, positioned on a sweatshirt. Always try to maintain your body in its quality temperature. Don't neglect approximately, in case you're sick, you voice is honestly too.

five.Warm Up

We want to stretch and loosen up the muscle businesses in advance than we sing, in simplest the identical manner as we'd in advance than a physical exercising. It is probably tempting to bypass it, however without warn up your voice might be wispy and flat right away. A mild warmness up loosens the vocal muscle tissues, gets rid of extra mucus and decreases the threat of damage. Don't go to the outer parameters of your voice notwithstanding the truth that; some slight exercising like buzzing will do the trick.

6.No Shouting

Raising your voice unexpectedly will positioned a massive strain for your vocal cords if you haven't warmed up. Sometimes we want to because of our every day challenges and sports activities like searching for to save you a touch infant from getting on a hectic tarred road with plenty of massive and small vehicles passing however you're an extended manner away. But the key's being aware.

7.Healthy Eating

A diet that promotes everyday proper health can also be superb to your voice. Fresh stop end result and veggies incorporate excessive water content fabric cloth and a meals that hydrates you could assist your vocal cord. Try and keep away from claggy dairy like chocolate, it creates mucous.

eight.Remedy Drink

A mug of heat water with lemon, ginger and honey is a incredible herbal tonic for the throat. The Vitamin C in lemon cleanses and cuts thru phlegm, the ginger reduces irritation and honey soothes and lubricates the vocal cords. Avoid caffeinated drink like energy beverages.

9.Sore Throat Care

A tender throat or a not unusual cold obtained't usually advocate no creating a song, however if your voice is hurting, it needs greater relaxation and hydration. Lozenges (Vitamin C) can assist earlier than a gig or rehearsal however keep away from the anesthetic type that numbs; you want on the manner to enjoy your throat or you can do extra harm.

10.Steaming

Steaming is an powerful and easy way to alleviate a sore throat and unfasten mucous within the nose, throat and lungs permitting you to sing extra pretty simply even as the voice is suffering.

CHAPTER 5: Vocal Dynamics

Using numerous dynamics while creating a tune can extensively enhance your overall performance. Singing dynamics are a tool that all artists can use to deliver a everyday overall performance alive, carry emotion and save you their common normal overall performance from being static.

Vocal (singing) dynamics is the exercise of controlling vocal volumes. It goes beyond absolutely creating a song loud or quiet. It moreover consists of creating a tune vowels and phrases at the best quantity. Dynamics moreover embody silences and rests, which singers shouldn't overlook approximately approximately.

There are many techniques to encompass vocal dynamics into your traditional performance, from simple topics which embody developing volumes and sundry harmonics to converting phrases and transport.

Vocal Dynamics In Singing

'Messa di Voce' is a not unusual technique that dynamic singers use to enhance their vocals. Messa di Voce is an Italian announcing that translates as placing of voice. It pertains to how a performer can sing in a slow crescendo and decrescendo on an extended sustained tone.

In exercise, a dynamic singer will begin making a song quietly, grade by grade developing the volume at the same time as keeping a easy vocal, then bringing the vocals backtrack again.

Vocal Dynamics Definition

Firstly, allow's start with what it way; the definition of vocal dynamics derives from the Greek word Dynamo. This translates as Power. In musical phrases, we define vocal dynamics in making a tune as being the volume of the voice. This can relate to the variation amongst notes.

How well you use dynamics to enhance their voice and ordinary performance is an hassle of manipulate. A microphone will nice get you up to now, because the maximum expert singers inside the global are capable of challenge their voice during a room without the want for amplification.

How To Improve Vocal Dynamics When Singing

Singing dynamics is a phrase frequently misunderstood. In the context of vocals, it equates to how the fantastic at which you can transfer from soft to loud making a track. A dynamic singer is able to create a standard average overall performance as a way to set them aside from the amateurs. If you may grasp dynamics for your making a song, it's miles going to help you challenge depth, feeling and a similarly layer for your vocal general overall performance.

five Key Tools Of Vocal Dynamics

1.Increase/Decrease Vocal Volume

This is whilst dynamic singers can use to help the emotion from the music encounter during their standard overall performance. Many singers pick to growth the quantity in their vocals once they hit the maximum emotional part of the music, however moreover do not forget lowering the quantity at fantastic points because it emphasizes the elements in which you boom the quantity.

The key right here is to differ your quantity at some point of the tune and change up your vocal dynamics.

2.Articulate Through Characterization

If you're making a song a satisfied a part of a track, try to mirror that during your vocal dynamics. Although it could no longer necessarily healthy with the track as a whole, it's going to offer an extra dynamic to your overall performance.

three.Change Vowel Shape

It can regularly be tough to find techniques to make your sing stand out. Changing vowel shape can be a diffused manner to do this. A right example is announcing me as might also additionally additionally in the appropriate music; this could subtly add some aspect unique to the general overall performance and make your vocal dynamic super.

4.Add Silence/Rests

Of course, in the course of your normal overall performance, you want to be making a song for max of it, however occasionally such as silences or rests makes the subsequent vocals sound extra remarkable and affords extra drama to your vocal dynamics and normal performance.

five.Phrasing

Extending a phrase in desire to maintaining it brief and taking a breath can regularly offer a modern day dynamic to the performance and can help to show off your vocals.

Note: It is not vital to attempt to use a majority of these dynamics in a single basic performance; if you try and use all of them, you danger the overall performance sounding too messy.

It is critical to enlarge using dynamics within the route of your average general performance. Singing the verse and the chorus in the equal way sooner or later of the tune is clearly going to grow to be repetitive, so that you want to appearance to feature some dynamics to keep away from the overall performance being best a loop of the number one verse and refrain, which can turn out to be quite whole and stupid.

It is vital to take into account that now not all of these vocal dynamics may be suitable for each singer's style of vocal. It is smart to realise which of them match your vocals and which ones don't work on your vocal.

The Ear

Our notion of sound relies upon at the organic system we are born with—our ears and our brains. Sound includes strain fluctuations in a medium (as an example, the air). The stress fluctuation enters the ear via the ear canal that ends with the eardrum. Vibrations at the eardrum are carried to the Cochlea by using manner of 3 tiny bones—the Malleus, Incus and

Stapes (together called the Ossicle). A vibration at the Ossicle produces sound waves which motive the basilar membrane to vibrate. These vibrations are transformed into electric powered impulse inside the auditory nerve, which carries data approximately the sound to the mind.

The ear is pretty touchy to sounds. The thoughts then strategies the electric alerts from the Cochlea using extremely complex networks of specialized neutrons in the thoughts. The way the sound is analyzed is predicated upon on our private non-public revel in to a positive volume.

The Ear As A Musical Tool

Do you apprehend that the ear can sing? You may be amazed to pay interest that they, in reality, have the ability to make specifically particular performers and contemporary check has found the real functionality of the ears interior musical creativity.

A properly performer can perform required responsibilities reliably and with out errors. In many respects, the very honest nature of the ear's responses to advantageous sounds consequences in the ear proving to be a totally dependable performer as its behavior can be predicted and so it is easily controlled. In the context of the listening gadget, the internal ear has the capability to behave as a fantastically effective device which could create its non-public sounds which experimental musicians were the usage of to show the listener's ears into taking factor performers in the cognizance of their track.

Figure 1: Diagram of the amazing factors of the ear.

Ear Training

Even if you have never heard of the time period ear training, if you have completed as a musician or have ever taken a track lesson, the possibilities are that you have labored on ear schooling.

Aural Skills are musical listening skills that develops your functionality to pay attention mainly with regards to track and sound, and ear education is the machine of developing those capabilities. For instance, if you will be privy to a track on the radio and play or sing it once more, you have been training your ears. If you may play lower decrease back a rhythm or can inform the difference amongst great sorts of sound results, you've got were given been training your ears.

Ear Training Exercise

Developing your Ural abilities with ear education blessings you in some of strategies which include enhancing reminiscence, developing self warranty a, growing your capacity to improvise and exercise your voice and tonation.

Here is an smooth ear training workout

1) Turn on the radio to a acquainted tune

2) Listen to the song for a couple of minutes

three) Now turn off the radio

four) Can you consider hearing the melody in your head?

5) Now attempt to hum the melody out loud

Congratulations, you really practiced ear schooling.

This unique capability is known as Audiation (the capability to hold a musical sound at the identical time because the sound is now not present). You can take this ear schooling exercising one step similarly through gambling another time the melody to your device or making a song the phrases; you are developing your musical ears and your musical memory.

10 Ear Training Tips For Beginners

As person beginners in music, you'll be concerned that your ears are not as developed as they would be in case you'd started out quicker. Don't worry! You can increase your ears with ear training at any time in your existence and a musician who starts offevolved offevolved past due and actively practices ear training can with out problem end up with far better ears than a musician who commenced younger but not noted ear education.

1. Start Simple: Learn Active Listening

Don't worry approximately being a Mozart in day one! Start with easy ear schooling sports.

Take a lesson from composer John Cage and Pauline Oliveros: near your eyes to soak up your sound surroundings.

Ask yourself questions like:

1) What do you pay interest? Work on differentiating amongst low sounds, excessive sounds, talking, animal noises, machines and so on.

2) Are the rhythms rapid or gradual?

3) Are the sounds loud or quiet?

4) Where are the sounds placed? Are they above you or beneath you?

Becoming aware of your environment (environment) like this enhances your aural abilities and it's miles an workout you may do ordinary

2. Test Your Hearing

If you find that you have trouble hearing humans talk in crowded rooms, can't pay attention excessive pitches, or must constantly ask human beings to copy themselves, then you truely could probable want to test your taking note of.

Check out the Action on Hearing Loss internet websites for a web listening to check and are seeking out recommendation from your clinical doctor.

If you're capable of experience the song you listen to, that's a fantastic sign your ears are still sturdy sufficient to emerge as an succesful music-maker! Testing your hearing is a good manner to verify this and will will let you understand if there are any troubles to be aware of as you studies song.

3. Test Your Existing Listening Skills

How well are your ears? You may recognize more than !

Take a easy Intro to Ear Training Quiz and discover your ear training degree. From there you may pursue the ear training which you want.

4. Let Rhythm Guide Your Learning

Although people consider rhythm as a natural ability, the fact is that your rhythm capabilities may be learnt and advanced. Honing your rhythmic abilities is frequently one of the quality procedures to start your ear training adventure. Almost each person can clap collectively with a favorite tune. Visit EasyEarTraining.Com and test your rhythm capabilities with a few rhythm quiz.

5. Master The Melody

Improving your musical experience of relative pitch is the crucial issue to statistics melody and studying a way to sing and understand intervals is a brilliant manner to try this. Download the free step and 1/2 of: first steps app to research the basics of c program languageperiod education.

6. Step Up To The Harmony

Once you are cushty with rhythm and melody, have fun with chords (Harmony). Chords are made ofor extra notes sounding collectively. Check the following financial break on harmony.

7. Have Ear Training Fun With A Friend

Music is continuously greater amusing with a chum. Rope for your choir or band next time you discern on a harmony exercising. Go on-line and take free courses on ear schooling collectively along with your partner.

8. Connect Your Ear Training With Your Instrument Or Singing Practice

Apply your new ear training talents on your instrumental or vocal skills. After some weeks, you can find out that your advanced ear education has absolutely extra your musicianship.

9.Learning About Audio

Ear training as an man or woman newbie doesn't truely contain rhythm, melody and concord. For those involved in music production or overall performance, studying the difference between unique audio effects and a manner to recognize frequencies are beneficial talents.

Do you apprehend the difference amongst reverb and echo? I assume many don't understand

How do you EQ your band's new demo?

Developing your ear for audio frequencies and consequences gives a valuable counterpart to musical ear schooling.

10. Keep Challenging Yourself

Once you have moved past rhythm, melody, concord or audio outcomes, keep to venture your self. Pick a modern-day day location and stretch your ears in a specific course. Learn a manner to dictate complex harmonic progressions, teach your self sound synthesis or compose true tune. There are limitless ways to move beyond the basics and turn out to be an ear training guru.

Scoring A Song

Firstly, all and sundry who is musically talented can score track. But not every body gifted can score track efficiently. Because scoring songs effectively includes listening to all the facts in a music. And moreover, now not anybody desires to go through the painstaking manner of scoring. For the truth which you are taking element in the tune and singing alongside doesn't imply you've got were given scored the music.

Some singers who do now not recognize what it manner to acquire a music think it begins and end at listening to the song and studying its lyrics. Scoring a music appreciably depends to your degree in track, listening speedy, technicality of the music. You don't score a music anyhow; it desires ATTENTION and CONCENTRATION. Now the huge questions are:

A)What does scoring a music suggest?

B)How can I rating a song successfully?

SCORING A SONG is the act of analyzing how a tune come to be written, structured, produced and moreover the capability to interpret equal flawlessly or taking identical to any other degree. Meaning that, you want to realise the lyrics, harmony, melody, rhythm and plenty of others. You can inversely become the owner and manufacturer of that track.

CHAPTER 6: How Can I Score A Song Effectively

I actually have 9 factors that in quick and informatively explains the way to efficiently rating a track.

1.Listen

Get your phone or mp3 player, take note of the song, and revel in the melody. Don't start studying it. Feel the weight and beauty of the track. Listen as often as feasible.

2.Know The Structure Of The Song

Establish the critical factor of the tune. Then recognise the way it started out out each from Intro to chorus, from chorus to verse to the refrain to the bridge to vamp and otherwise. This will assist you purchased loads at the longer term. This is the primary level of scoring a track as it offers you the outline and prediction had to short studying.

3.Write The Lyrics

Getting the lyrics down on a pocket e-book/notepad will help you whilst learning the lyrics. It is ideal to pass-test the lyrics, however pay attention to it if it tallies to what you are taking note of. You perhaps paying attention to vision and seeing assignment on line. I don't advice you need to go to the net and replica n paste. Be very cautious approximately that.

4.Learn All Vocal Parts, Breaks and so on.

This is in which I now and again start to have trouble with my choir. You pay attention a few say, I'm an Alto singer, so I scored best the Alto factor; but to increase in a choir enterprise, you want to analyze all components. You are a singer and not simply an Alto singer. Beside, the song director would probably determine to alternate the important thing of the track which may also have an effect on the components. Singers need to furthermore understand a manner to swap components. Know whilst each detail is to be had in, once they sing melody or concord. Also be aware of the dynamics (crescendos, decrescendos) in the track.

As you rating, ensure you're jotting down subjects. Make certain you change what you are reading into solfas notation. Hence, education on transcribing track to tonic solfas is usually recommended for every body within the choir. But in case you could't do that for now, you could report what you've scored via a recorder for destiny motive. The dullest pen is higher than the sharpest mind.

5.Be The Lead Singer (Soloist) And The Backup Singers

Try as a good deal as viable to benefit the lead vocal aspect and the backups. This help you enlarge musically and moreover assist you correct others; even the lead singer at the same time as she or he flops. Learn everything collectively with the adlibs. As you score specific gifted humans, you can find your non-public expression very quickly.

6.Learn The Instrumentation Sound

Don't say you don't realize the manner to play, learn the sound. The keyboardist might not get the melody or solo issue. You can describe what you've heard. Scoring the instrumentation sound moreover broadens your song thoughts. Knowing the sound arrangements will help you recognize the way to glide better on the song.

7.Sing Along

You sing alongside facet with the music or song even if you have no longer or have perfected the music. Try making a track the equal aspect you pay attention in the song. Your voice texture ought to probably range however strive doing it at the side of your non-public voice texture. You is probably scoring Kierra Sheard's track even as your voice texture is like Eben. Do it in any case.

eight.Try To Sing Without Listening Or Playing The Song

This is in that you understand when you have been joking because you started out out the scoring system. This will reveal you to areas in which you haven't perfected at the same time as scoring. It can even expose the lines you've no longer gotten, melodies you've no longer mastered. Most folks will be predisposed to sing well with musical gadgets however cast off the beat, we sound quack. Note in which you are making mistakes and float lower again to the song and accurate yourself. Put the ones locations at the loop (repeat) till you have got mastered them.

9. Own The Song

There's no manner you can perform your splendid from a track that you haven't scored or perfected with all of the recommendations given above. We stated earlier that scoring a song manner you to start with comprehend all of the systems, lyrics and manufacturing of the song, then you both reflect equal or perform your non-public (own the music). Your information of scoring a tune makes it much less complicated an extraordinary way to won the track. If you may make the track yours, then you truely have taken the tune to each other stage.

With those few suggestions, you can score any tune successfully with out fear.

Harmony

A solo melody line may be catchy, but there can be a completely unique aura sensation while extra notes sound concurrently with the melody. These additional notes function as harmony and they're able to redecorate a piece of track.

What Is Vocal (Singing) Harmony?

Vocal or developing a music harmony includes supplementing a vocal melody with extra notes that suits the underlying chord shape.

Vocal concord is a style of song whereby a set of singers sing a hard and fast of consonant notes composing the precept melody. The basic sound of the melody is Fuller and extra complex, giving it an nearly ethereal (out of the arena) vibe. Singing in concord can enhance your over all vocal capabilities. It will will let you test with one-of-a-type patterns and tones and is certain to make you a extra flexible singer, that is generally welcome for those who are searching out to pursue a musical profession. Singing Harmony may additionally improve your ears and your song listening to. Not all singers are born to be lead vocalists, but making a music concord can considerably beautify your opportunities of landing gigs. Whatever your motivation, never be afraid to experiment along with your tune and try new subjects–along side the incorporation of harmony.

How Can I Sing Harmony?

There is not any single massive method for analyzing this making a song functionality. Some singers actually have a high aptitude for spotting pitches and don't require lots exercise; at the same time as others should probable want hours and hours of ear education to apprehend the idea well.

1. Learn Basic Music Theory

You don't need to comprehend each problem of tune concept to be a wonderful singer, however it allows–a lots! By studying simple tune concept, you will better apprehend the mind that deliver tune to existence, learn how to apprehend intervals and discover ways to paintings on training your ear, a essential step for any developing singer.

Harmony Singing calls for a clean know-how of musical intervals. While some might be capable of draw close this in simple terms through the use of ear, the reality is that most of the singers need to educate their ears to apprehend why they are doing topics as they do. Regardless of which corporation you belong to, making an investment time into gaining knowledge of important song idea will make you a greater flexible musician and allow draw close new idea speedy.

2. Intervals: The Heart Of Harmony Singing

Intervals represent the gap many of the two notes on a musical scale, along with number one and minor versions. This reachable list of periods offers you a quick examine of the kinds of periods that exist. A distance amongfirst and the very last tone on a prime scale is referred to as an octave. The names of durations of the important scale as a consequence supply names as a consequence.

3. Chords: Shortcuts To Harmony

Chords are organization of notes finished concurrently, generating a uniform sound. The key to facts chords is to discover ways to construct them. For example, foremost chords usually encompass a prime phrase, a number one 0.33 and a amazing fifth.

There are numerous different styles of chords, which includes chord triads:

a) Major chords

b) Minor chords

c)Augmented chords

d) Diminished chords

e) Seventh chords. To call some

If you understand the chords, it is simple to perceive the notes a great way to wholesome in great concord with the essential be privy to the tune inside the melody. It all is going again to know-how primary music idea and making use of it to your creating a track.

4. Timing Is Essential

I can not overemphasize the significance of timing in making a song harmony. Even if all of the singers in the group are on-pitch and comprehend their intervals, the feel of concord can be out of region in the event that they don't sing at the identical tempo and timing. Instead, the creating a tune will sound messy and uncoordinated. It is very vital so you can find out the clues in any song and time your the front because of this. It takes a bit of workout, however when you are used to locating those clues in the melody, your timing may be on its manner to impeccable.

Some of the maximum common technique to locating out the hassle of timing encompass attentive being attentive to the rhythm phase of the song; mist mainly the drums and percussions. They provide structure and frame to the music.

5. Practice In Group

If you're making prepared to sing in concord with others, you have to spend time working in the direction of with them. You can discover ways to sing harmony by myself at domestic, the use of recording but it's not usually the same in real lifestyles. Singers have taken into consideration one of a type fashion possibilities and loads of quirks that might effects throw off your timing. Practicing with extraordinary singers will assist you gather chemistry and a better understanding of your function in the organisation's universal overall performance. It may additionally offer you with a motivation raise and a revel in of achievement as you hone your craft and sound with colleagues. It is likewise a really perfect possibility to get some recommendation and mentoring from special singers. The element of mentoring in tune can't be neglected.

6. Listen, Listen, Listen

Always try to mimic the greats. Spending limitless hours being attentive to songs through mythical artists that employs concord will help you better is aware of its fee and significance, similarly to gaining a more thorough knowledge of the way songs are composed. Learning is a non-forestall technique and there are usually better and greater advanced singers who will allow you to develop.

One of the most effective methods to spend it sluggish taking note of music is through choosing some songs with terrific harmonies that you virtually enjoy. Play a tune again and again as you try to come to be aware of the dominant melody, concord, periods and chords in the songs. The extra time you spend with song, the much less complicated it's going to in all likelihood be so that it will draw near new idea and pick out out up new techniques as you increase your voice and music acumen.

7. Practice Makes Perfect

Very few humans are born with a herbal aptitude or capability to imitate pitch and tones or pick up complex tune mind through ear. Most folks need to artwork tough to beautify as singers and administrators however we furthermore need to paintings clever. The getting to know technique has numerous components, together with self-assessment, reflected image and motivation. Learning a way to sing harmony or factors isn't any unique. You want to begin at the beginning and undertake a systematic approach to mastering it. Be sure first of all easy songs an awesome way to allow and help you understand the technique rapid teaching you the way to understand melody, harmony, intervals and chords. Once you observe the ones essential thoughts, you may begin to workout them to extra complicated songs.

And also keep in mind that getting to know to sing concord is a tool. Don't get discouraged. Nobody learns the manner to sing in a single day. It requires ardour, region, determination (willpower) in addition to the need to push you mentally. Progress is a journey and those who're taking the adventure to harmony frequently have hassle seeing the consequences right away. Step decrease back every now and then and test what you have were given finished. Record your creating a song exercise and you'll beautify progressively.

Rhythm

Attempts to outline rhythm in music have produced an entire lot war of words, in detail due to the fact rhythm has often been identified with one or greater of it's constitutes, however not entirely separate, factors which incorporates accessory, metre and pace.

Rhythm in music is the vicinity of sounds in time.

The belief of rhythm moreover incurs in specific arts (e.G. Poetry, portray, sculpture and form) similarly to in nature (e.G. Organic rhythms).

CHAPTER 7: Elements of Rhythm

Unlike a painting or piece of sculpture which is probably compositions in region, a musical paintings is a composition mounted upon time. Whatever different factors a given piece of tune can also additionally additionally have (e.G. Patterns in pitch or timbre); rhythm is one critical element of all track. Rhythm can exist without melody, as in drumbeats of so-referred to as primitive song, however melody can't exist without rhythm. In music that has both concord and melody, the rhythmic shape can't be separated from them.

1.Beat

A unit branch of musical time is called a beat. Just as one is privy to the frame's consistent pulse or heartbeat, so in composing, acting or taking note of music, one is privy to a periodic succession of beat.

2.Tempo

The tempo of crucial beat is called tempo. The expressions, sluggish pace and brief tempo suggest the life of a tempo that is 'neither gradual nor fast' however as an alternative mild. A moderate tempo is assumed to be that of a herbal walking pace (70 – 80 paces constant with minute).

The pace of a chunk of song indicated through the composer is but neither absolute nor very last. In performance, it's far in all likelihood to trade because of issues which includes the size and reverberation of the hall, the scale of the ensemble and the sonority of the units. A change within such limits does not have an impact on the rhythmic form of a tune piece.

3.Rubato

The pace of a chunk is neither inflexibly mathematical. It isn't feasible to stick in a musical way to the metronomic beat for any period of time. In a loosely knit passage, a decent or tensed tempo possibly required; on this sort of crowded passage, a slackening maybe desired. Such changes of pace, known as Tempo Rubato – I.E. "robbed time" – are part of the song's character. Rubato needs the framework of an rigid beat from which it may go away and to which it could pass decrease lower back.

four.Time

The mind apparently seeks a few organizing principle in the belief of music, and if a grouping of sounds isn't objectively gift it imposes in reality one in every of its very own. Experiments indicates that the thoughts instinctively institution normal and identical sounds into twos and threes, stressing each 2nd or 0.33 beat and therefore creates from an in any other case monotonous series a succession of sturdy and vulnerable beats, so timing can be very crucial for a musician.

Types Of Rhythm

1. Random Rhythm

In a random rhythm, the elements or components of a chunk are organized and repeated and no longer the use of a genuine normal intervals. The elements that make up the music can also additionally in reality appear out of region or disorganized; but successfully however deliver a nice sound if the composer is aware about what they may be doing. When listening to a quick part of the song or sound, the notes and rests sample may seem random, till it is listened to in its entirety.

2. Regular Rhythm

A tune with a regular rhythm basically follows the identical pattern or intervals over and over all over again. The whole piece is generally really the identical loop repeating for the complete period of the song, as desired with the beneficial aid of the producer. Regular rhythms also can begin to sound monotonous, but there are super songs that have been written and recorded with this form of rhythm.

3. Alternating Rhythm

When a song has a regular rhythmic pattern and there appears to be a want to interrupt it off the monotonous sound spectrum it possesses, growing alternating rhythms may be a solution. Just as the call implies, alternating rhythm takes place whilst a music haseveryday rhythms alternating sequentially. Depending at the composer, there are definitely one of a kind elements of rhythm that can be used to accumulate this, from the only alternating sample amongstmelody lines to a extra complex pattern switching among precise rhythms.

4. Flowing Rhythm

Flowing rhythm is one that could on occasion be defined as religious. Think of the sounds that originate from a flowing River or the pattern of rain falling. There are not any precise depictions of notes and rests durations in this form of rhythm, simplest a persistent flowing piece that includes a halt while the tune stops.

5. Progressive Rhythm

A modern rhythm is made thru way of truely changing one element of a improvement at a time as it repeats. As the development transcends, notable little factors or characters are modified or introduced to offer the whole piece a cutting-edge experience, constructing pride proper from the begin of the tune constantly until it receives to it's height.

Rhythm in ultra-modern is most effective a sample in location and time. For track, it is a pattern of musical activities, factors, notes and rests in time. A lot of rhythm kinds are based on a cyclic or periodic pattern or repetition of activities. These are typically categorised as metric rhythms and the duration of repetition is referred to as the degree bar. Metric rhythm involves the subdivision of bar into identical gadgets marked with the useful resource of a pulse, called beat. Non-metric rhythm doesn't placed the ones unique divisions and stuck durations into play. They sincerely arise additively.

Importance of Rhythm

In this have a have a observe, the situation of rhythm has been stated and multiple factors that assist us to understand what rhythm is ready in song have been hooked up. These factors cut throughout one of a kind elements of tune idea, and help offer an normal meaning to the concept of rhythm and its simple significance in tune.

Even even though we already comprehend that rhythm is a crucial element in tune, we've not been able to pinpoint a number of its significance in a easy and understandable way. We can't just say some thing is important without being capable of list its usefulness.

In track, rhythm serves because the riding strain that propels a chunk earlier and gives a composition shape. The people of an ensemble may now not be able to maintain time without the underlying beat, time signature and pace. The rhythm phase of maximum musical ensembles is accountable for imparting the company's simple rhythmic framework. So having an first rate revel in of rhythm as a musician, and having the functionality to feel and keep a regular pace places you halfway thru the adventure of turning into a first-rate musician.

Chapter 8: Getting Started and What To Expect

Singing a hundred and one

You will learn how to put together your hobby earlier than you start exercising. For example you may want to set a time for exercise that doesn't interfere together along with your ingesting time desk. You wouldn't need to sing on a complete stomach of meals due to the fact it may cause a lazy overall performance. I inspire you to have your meal about an hour or a half of hour before you start. That manner your meals is digested and out of the manner and not actually sitting to your belly geared up to be processed. You will learn how to do matters singers do ordinary to put together themselves for growing a track engagements or performances. It doesn't matter number if you are self taught or reading with a expert vocal trainer. You can be given the

'the way to's' needed to put together you for your vocal endeavors.

This ebook will help you with becoming a greater assured singer. It isn't designed to teach you everything about making a song. Yet you may gain sensible information inside the capacity to demonstrate real approach, shape and sound extremely good. .

Your Image of You.

What this segment of the e-book in brief specializes in is more of a highbrow thing of approaches you can need to go through in thoughts viewing your voice, and the sounds it makes, for the most effective very last results. What do you observed you sound like? I'm positive we've all had a person touch upon the manner they assume our voice sounds to them. Well, if so, then we also can have developed a concept of methods we recognize our voice primarily based at the accolades of others and/or the terrible remarks. Either way I'm here to share with you a completely particular point of method. Understand this: out of the billions upon billions of beings born upon this beautiful earth, you are uniquely and splendidly made. Your voice is the best one you can ever acquire. Accept it and discover it irresistible. The sounds you're making are yours and that they've been made to suit into the rest of the lovely sounds of this universe. If you could get in which I'm coming from with this assertion, you're directly to a few detail massive on the side of your voice. Embrace it and develop it. Don't disgrace your voice via saying smooth things like: "'I can't sing" or " I sound terrible" truely primarily based simply upon someone else's thoughts of your voice or your very own self doubt. Always recollect, a splendid technique can supply a pleasing final results. Otherwise, you are doing a disservice on your present. Instead, artwork on improving your abilities. We all want to do that. In doing so, you may accomplish development in making your singing voice sound better.

Chapter 9: Singing with Proper Body Alignment

Breathing

Let's speak approximately breath in advance than we get into posture. Breath is what gives us earthly beings our existence pressure. Okay, I'm sure every body agree that we want breath to live, correct? Singing requires us to apply proper breathing. If we use breath within the proper manner, we're able to sing a music without a trouble. If we use it incorrectly, we can battle through even a easy phrase in a track. So pretty obviously, we ought to recognition at the energy of breath that is being pulled upon at the equal time as we talk and sing. Breath is a pal to the vocalist. We need to use as a exceptional deal breath as desired whilst we are creating a music. As a vocal teach it is my mission to train students to breathe nicely while singing. For example, you wouldn't want to be bending over or slouched over while you are trying to sing a tune, because you may block the airway from successfully projecting your sound great. Instead, you will want to be recognition up right now simply so the breath can float out easily. Knowing whilst to take a breath is also crucial to the singer due to the truth it is able to make or destroy how properly you sound on the same time as making a music your tune. You never need to sound like you are walking out of breath in the center of a tune or word. Nor should you want to sound "winded", as despite the fact that you're going to crumble in advance than finishing the phrase. The sound incredible, irrespective of how easy or loud, need to be full and virtually controlled. A wonderful exercise is to take a breath at some point of every four-eight counts or beats consistent with measure of the tune. I will provide an example under of a super vocal workout I use to help students studies wherein to take their breaths inside the route of a music.

Exercise 1:

Take the music "Mary Had A Little Lamb". Sing it exactly the way you are analyzing it to complete this exercise. Inhale a deep breath and sing out multi feature breath for four region take a look at beats (counts)...

Sing:

Ma ry Had A...

Do that every one in one breath.

Then take some one-of-a-kind breath and sing:

Lit tle Lamb

Do that each one in a unmarried breath

Inhale a few different breath and sing:

Lit tle lamb

Do that every one in a unmarried breath

Inhale some different breath and sing:

Inhale all over again and entire the word:

Lit tle lamb

This workout is completed on a 4 depend the use of 4/4 time signature this means that that 4 area be aware beats in step with degree.

The reason of this exercising is to expose you the manner to practice taking in breaths after each quick phrase. A phrase is normally one to 2 measures lengthy. Practice this over and over till it turns into 2d nature. You can begin first by using using manner of just clapping at a steady pace. As you're clapping, begin to recall from one to 4, then circulate lower returned to 1 and repeat the trouble all over again. Next, begin creating a tune the primary line. Then keep the rest of the workout on the same pace. This manner you'll experience the phrases synchronize with the beat. This exercise allows to show you in which to take proper breaths at the give up of every word.

Exercise 2:

You will use the equal tune "Mary Had A Little Lamb" for this workout. Sing the tune exactly the manner it's miles written. Inhale a deep breath and sing out for eight beats (counts)...This will let you train your self on a way to inhale each eight beats or counts constant with word.

Sing:

Ma ry had A... Lit tle Lamb

Do that each one in a unmarried breath.

Then take every one of a kind breath and sing:

Lit tle lamb… Lit tle Lamb

This exercise is performed on an eight remember which incorporates eight location be aware beats. That is measures with 4 beats in every.

You have just sung, Mary Had A Little Lamb (on an eight do not forget). That need to be executed multi function breath. Practice this 4-8 times.

You need to continually recollect to depend upon the breath to maintain you thru a phrase. Taking one breath to sing a full eight bar phase without a doubt is the goal! Make smart breath alternatives. If you sense yourself out of breath take every other one at that precise point. Follow the ones commands and you will become accurate at taking breaths in amongst phrases correctly.

A couple of steps to consider on the same time as focusing at the breath:

1. Awareness of your body equals mindfulness of breath. Duration and period equals how extended your inhalation is and how prolonged your exhalation may be. You can adjust and have a look at these items through recognition and focusing on the breath as you are breathing in and out.

2. Practice growing your volume of breath consumption. You can do this thru measuring how an lousy lot air it takes to top off and increase your lungs even as you're inhaling. For example, you'll inhale and start counting alongside to your head or hands. This will diploma how lengthy it takes to top off your lungs with air. It is fine to do that even as fame. The purpose is on the manner to inhale as a bargain as 12-16 counts.

Exercise 3:

1.   Stand right away, with toes shoulder width apart. Place your arms on your belly. Take in a breath. Begin to gauge the depth of the breath collectively along with your arms on your stomach. Watch how your arms will pass internal and out as you inhale and exhale. As you're monitoring the air stepping into and out, word how it's also touring all within the course of your frame. This breathing technique want to reason a chilled sensation. Each time you try this, you will look at increasingly the manner to modify the breath. You will learn how to maintain longer notes and breath with a good deal a great deal less try.

2.   Inhale through the nose to create an opening and growth of the chest; exhale through the mouth to deflate and drop the chest. Also, as you are doing this you will be preserving a regular rely or beat. You will now not need to place hobby at the

depend variety. Stay focused at the breath and allow the depend come sincerely similar to the beat of your coronary coronary heart.

3.   Focus on the length of breath. Duration offers with the period of time you are able to hold your breath in addition to the quantity. You need to increase the pressure. This allows you to build up your respiration great. Your strain growth seems some thing like whilst you're blowing air right right into a balloon and the quantity of air forces it to growth outward. You experience whilst air is going into your lungs down past your chest into the stomach location elevating up the diaphragm. Envision this taking place as you are reading a way to do it.

Posture

This is enormously vital for the singer. Your sound splendid will rely on how properly you are the usage of posture to assist your notes and breath. You don't need to be slouched over or bent within the incorrect position while you are trying to sing because of the reality the sound can be stricken by it. You moreover don't need to dam your sound from popping out of your mouth sincerely. Putting pressure inside the incorrect areas of your frame will intervene with sound exceptional sooner or later of making a song. Stand immediately up collectively along with your knees slightly bent just so they aren't in a locked function. Then take a deep breath and sing out. You need your neck to be right away and your head going through beforehand. Your once more want to additionally be right away, no longer slouched inward. You do not need your head to be returned and face in the direction of the ceiling because of the reality you could not be able to successfully manipulate your respiratory that manner. The tremendous sound first rate will encompass correct posture.

The Head Voice

What does it virtually propose while people say 'sing out of your head voice' ? This is truely regarding the location of the sound resonating off of your vocal chords. It will experience similar to the sound is coming from the top of your head due to the truth you could sense a robust vibration to your better frame and in particular to your head even as the notes are being sung. It additionally refers to your vocal range and the place it resonates from at the same time as you are making a song the excessive notes. It's crucial to realize that the top voice is more potent than the falsetto voice. It is your vocal chords doing most of the artwork, not surely your head. But whilst you sing and are hitting your excessive notes, it feels similar to the sound or vibration is to your head. That is likewise due to the fact the sound is traveling in an upward position in the direction of the pinnacle of your mouth hole space. So, each time you pay interest a person say, sing from your "head voice" you may recognize what that means.

An instance of the top voice is Lizzo's "Truth Hurts ". In the hole line she says " Why men notable…" It appears like a belt sensation and the position is ahead within the the the the the front of the mouth.

It's now not to be burdened in conjunction with your falsetto. Although falsetto notes are without a doubt high they're additionally very breathy and airy. Plus your falsetto may be felt in both your chest vicinity in addition to the pinnacle.

The Chest Voice

The chest voice is usually the vicinity in which shallow breaths are taken and sang from. Your chest voice is especially felt inside the throat place. It is in which the speakme voice is felt the weakest for the purpose that strain and stress is typically placed on the vocal cords because of awful breath placement. The sound may be nasal for some human beings. The chest voice isn't to be confused with the sound you will get even as you are respiration properly from your diaphragm. It isn't the maximum comfortable vicinity to sing from, however often green singers revert to that area of breath placement.

This isn't the maximum comfortable area to sing from. The placement of the breath is taken into consideration wrong and, often, dangerous. It may be very one-of-a-kind from singing from the diaphragm.

Chapter 10: Singing from the Diaphragm

Vibration and Tones

There is a distinction a number of the chest and the diaphragm? Singing from the diaphragm is even as the breath is coming from the lowest of the belly area. It is in which you experience maximum comfortable and cushty speakme from. This is commonly the lower take a look at in of the voice. The tone and textures are an awful lot deeper, fuller and richer. You will surely experience the vibration tones on your chest location while you sing notes however, the breath placement is inside the bottom of the diaphragm. You might also have the entire vocal cords vibrating and the diaphragm engaged while creating a tune and speaking.

The chest wall is where the ribs are positioned among distinct vital body factors. The muscle corporations a few of the ribs and determination are what increases the chest and lowers it. The breath flows downward into that area to permit the air to circulate and convey once more up exceptional or horrible sound, in quantity, relying for your body posture.

Exercise 4:

Breathe into your mouth and supply the air downward to the chest . Notice how your shoulders begin to boom up and outward. When that takes place you are the use of your chest in region of your diaphragm.

This is now and again called a shallow breath as it isn't in reality as sturdy due to the reality the diaphragm breath. You can get a few short and brilliant sounds while respiratory out of your chest however it isn't recommended for the motive that fullest and most supported sounds may be coming from taking in a large quantity of air and sending it right right down to your stomach- diaphragm area. This lets in the first-class of sound to be supported for the furthest distance and sound.

There is a few thing I name the Buddha Belly breath technique. I use it to show college students the way to sing absolutely while hitting the excessive notes in heaps tons less than half of-hour of normal practice. It's quite clean to do. Here is what you will do…

Exercise five:

1.   Stand tall along with your once more immediately however do now not lock your knees as this may limit the air because of the fact you're surely preserving in anxiety even as any a part of your body is "locked". You need to sense the natural go together with the float of air during your entire whole body.

2.   Next, inhale a deep breath and slowly permit it out. Do that 3 times to get warmed up.

3.   To hold, take a 'Buddha Belly Breath' thru breathing in in as lots air you may with out straining your rib cage. Allow your belly to poke out as a long way as it could move. Imagine the 'Buddha' at the identical time as you are doing this.

four.   Hold that for 2 counts then launch it on the sound of : Ahhhh Mmmm

five.   Be certain to open and close to your mouth three instances until you now not have any air left. Feel the air leaving your frame as your stomach deflates backpedal. Relax your shoulders into it.

6.   Now that your lungs are empty, begin all over again with the aid of taking in a deep breath. Repeat this step approximately nine times for wonderful effects.

Vocal Techniques

In this ebook I reputation on what I get hold of as true with the maximum essential strategies are for buying any amateur commenced out inside the right manner. That being stated, there are such a whole lot of particular and massive techniques to creating a track effectively. However allow's slim it down to three number one but important ones. The first goes to be hitting the excessive notes well. We use pressure, force and breath to attain as much as a excessive take a look at. We in no manner want to stress at the same time as doing so and this is why posture and proper breathing is taught up the the front. When you're making a song songs there are terms and dynamic adjustments all at some stage in the track. So we address one word at a time using the proper dynamics and breathing. Your method to a word is top. The beginning of the phrase, the center of the phrase and the completing of the phrase determines the overall phrase. When you begin the phrase you need to generally take a deep breath to begin. You want to be in the maximum comfortable kingdom of thoughts as feasible. You also can enjoy aggravating at the equal time as making a track within the front of a crowd and if that takes area hold in mind to respire and lighten up. You might also moreover use critical stress to provide the sound a few more extent. Remember the breathing method we mentioned in advance. Deep breath in and send it right all the way down to your diaphragm. Then slowly launch it on an exhale at the same time as allowing the tone to overlay the breath. While inside the center of the phrase, loosen up into the breath as you are making a song the terms. This prevents you from on foot out of breath and collapsing the study. Do now not strain the breath out even as growing a tune the word. Allow the sound to go with the float out and you may experience the breath and vibration as you keep and whole the word correctly. So, combine your inhale with the start of the word and release the terms over the tones.. The breath facilitates to preserve notes. This is some thing that need to be practiced regularly. Your nice strategies will most effective embody workout. You will see improvement and a change in your sound as you start to practice those and the opposite techniques.

Pitch and Diction

When you pay attention someone speakme about pitch in making a tune you automatically apprehend they may be regarding the immoderate and espresso frequencies of the vocal range. A person's voice tiers everywhere from a soprano, mezzo-soprano, alto, tenor, baritone on proper all the manner down to a bass. For instance, If you have a voice that is able to sing more excessive notes you'll maximum possibly be considered to have a soprano vocal range. . In the middle of the vocal tiers is the alto. At the lowest of the vocal variety is the tenor. And on the very low backside is the bass or baritone vocal range.

The vocal variety is some thing that may be informed to increase higher and lower. If you want to increase your vocal variety you want to practice doing so. Although you have been born together together with your precise sound, with schooling you may normally decorate it. Again, you need to train the voice if you need it to broaden. Musical scales are a superb way to help you in schooling the voice for higher pitch.

Diction found with the pitch is surprisingly important for a singer. Diction specializes within the manner the terms sound coming out of the mouth. This is important with growing a music because of the fact the manner you pronounce the phrase determines how properly it will sound to the ears of the listener. Therefore , you want your phrase to be understood while you're making a song. We will do a little examples with diction to get a richer records.

Take the ones vowels and say them slowly exactly as they will be written.

1. Say the A - Ah ay: Ah sound first and then upload the ay sound after.

2. Say the E - Eh ee: Eh sound first then upload the ee sound very last.

three. Say the I - Ee aye: Ee sound first then upload the aye sound very last

four. Say the O - Oh oo: Oh sound first then add the oo sound ultimate.

five. Say the U - Oo uh: Oo sound first then upload the uh sound final.

First exercise announcing every person vowel and enunciate with clean diction. Say the vowel with identical emphasis on each syllable (i.E Ah-ay). Do that severa instances to get your mouth and vocal chords all warmed up. Do now not cut up the sound.You need to preserve the be conscious count number range range for approximately four beats after which bypass on to the subsequent vowel until you have said all of them.

Second step is to duplicate the preceding steps with a sixty second loosen up duration in amongst. Then flow into at once to the following vowel and do the same for 6 - 9 instances until you have got accomplished all of them.

Lastly, make certain to start off in a very comfortable state. Resonate in your backside chest voice to start. This is the lowest pitch your voice is able to do effortlessly. Your vocal capability isn't always to be in comparison with every one-of-a-kind character. Your variety can be based totally to your private genetic make up and that is what determines how excessive or low your voice is going.

You will discover your variety with out difficulty through gambling notes on both a piano, keyboard or guitar. Go to any piano and find Middle C. This is likewise called C4 (the 4th C positioned at the keyboard). It is in the center 1/2 of most keyboards. Sit on the piano. Play the attention after which try to sing alongside to wholesome the sound you pay interest. If you're able to sing it really then your vocal variety sits somewhere internal that check in of the piano/ keyboard. If you find out your self struggling to sing the word then you definately genuinely definately want to transport on to the following be conscious at the keyboard. Sing until you hit the very notable phrase with out straining and then mark that spot.

A latest exercising for ladies's voices is to begin at Middle C on the keyboard and cross up closer to the right of the keyboard. A sizable workout for a man's voice is to begin at C4 and paintings down the dimensions within the direction of the left of Middle C. The higher notes are in the course of the right of Middle C and the lower notes are in the course of the left of Middle C. Either manner, to locate your correct range you can want to move up and down the dimensions. The purpose is to ensure no longer to damage your vocal cords with the useful resource of straining them in any other case you could do important harm. If you're cracking at the same time as creating a track a observe most probable you are not capable of sing that phrase and it's miles out of your vocal variety.

Look on the picture underneath. To assist you locate Middle C you may rely down 5 white keys beginning from the left of this photograph. It is the 5th white key some of the 3 black keys and the to white keys. .

Chapter 11: Keeping the Beat

Rhythm is Key

The rhythm is the beat, tempo and motion pattern your song will journey on the equal time as you sing. It isn't unusual to make up rhythm patterns the usage of 4 beats consistent with degree or 3 beats according to degree. Rhythm is in all kinds of tune. Your coronary coronary heart beats to a rhythm. Rhythm flows in some unspecified time in the future of the tune; It drives the existence pressure of the tune through vibration and tones. In music, rhythm enables create the natural cycle and changes which you pay attention at some stage in the music.

This exercising will awareness on rhythm through track. When you're making a music you have to go with the flow to and fro, or faucet your toes, or snap your fingers, or clap your hands. Whichever you choose out will sincerely assist to get a regular rhythm flowing before you start to start making a song along.

Exercise 6:

Start with the resource of tapping your toes at a regular tempo. Count out loud from 1-4. Repeat that count some times to get a ordinary tempo. Start creating a music the terms to "Row Row Row Your Boat". Don't prevent the rhythm and motion absolutely replace the numbers with the phrases. Sing that over and over a few instances until it starts offevolved offevolved to revel in comfortable. Play spherical with the pace of your rhythm at the same time as you sing the phrases. Get into the exercise of converting your tempo. You can select any song you want and do this exercise as part of your every day vocal heat up.

The Importance of Practice

They say practice makes satisfactory. Not precisely. It is true that remarkable exercising makes development. In order to have a look at any new potential and do it effectively you want to create and determine to training it. There isn't any manner round exercise at the same time as you are getting to know the way to sing and bring a first-rate tone. Practice will help you train and supply a lift for your vocal chords just like a person who practices how to make stronger and tone his body muscle tissues.

Dedicate yourself to a exercising ordinary and you may no longer be upset because of the truth your voice will provide you with once more what you placed into it. It permits you properly use your voice on the equal time as creating a tune and to keep away from injuries in the approach. You begin to study your voice's strengths , weaknesses, on the facet of growing your range. It is within the exercise in which you may research and discover the particular tones and textures of your voice! Below is a every day exercising guide you can begin using now. And don't forget about, every example stated within the previous chapters can and need to be introduced as a part of your exercising everyday.

This step by step exercise manual is designed to provide a every day vocal lesson warm up for proper body alignment and tone.

Chapter 12: Total Body Warm Up

Step 1. Stretch your fingers up within the air and Inhale. Extend your stomach out on the identical time as inhaling.

Step 2. Next as you're exhaling, bend over all the way all the manner all the way down to the floor as some distance as you could skip with out harming your again. If you feel tightness in the returned or lower legs prevent at that factor and go back once more up. Touch your toes if viable. Don't stress. Relax. Come lower lower returned up. While you're coming decrease again up, inhale a few distinctive deep breath. Stretch your fingers up inside the air again and repeat the previous step.

Step three. Repeat nine instances slowly

Exercise eight:

Total Body warmth up with sound

Step 1. Inhale a deep breath after which say the word HOO-ooo-ooo as you are exhaling all of the air out of your lungs. Listen to the body and the sound.

Step 2. Inhale a deep breath and then say the word "Nayyyyyyyy" as you are exhaling all of the air from your lungs. Don't overlook about to take note of the frame and sound.

Step 3. Do a few exceptional set of 9. You want to sense really snug.

Exercise 9:

Voice heat up

Step 1. Inhale a deep breath via your mouth and at the exhale say: hummm-ummmm Start at the low register of your voice and climb up the size to the pinnacle of the octave. Do this while preserving your mouth closed.

Step 2. After all of the air is about loose, take in a few different breath (If you're capable of sing to the subsequent octave maintain up to the following octave. If not, please circulate again to the start) and begin another time. Repeat nine instances.

The purpose is to educate your voice to transport from one octave to the second after which the 1/three resultseasily.

Exercise 10:

Volume and dynamics

Step 1. You can do that exercising in different procedures to add range and dynamics. Begin on a soft tone the number one time thru then go from smooth to medium.

Step 2. Go from loud to very loud. Make positive to mission your sound outward. Say those open vowels the usage of a big open mouth :

Naaaaaaa (begin smooth -then go up in amount)

Neeee (start easy -then skip up in quantity)

Niiiiiiiiiii (begin smooth -then float up in extent)

Nooooooo (start easy -then cross up in quantity)

Nuuuuuuu (begin smooth -then skip up in volume)

Chapter 13: Identifying Your Vocal Range

Bass, tenor, alto and soprano — those are the four easy levels of the human voice. Bass and tenor are usually attributed to the male human voice, at the same time as alto and soprano are attributed to the woman human voice. The bass range is commonly the non-public style of notes the male human voice can hit on the equal time due to the fact the tenor variety is the great. Similarly, the alto variety is the inner maximum style of notes the woman voice can hit at the equal time due to the fact the soprano range is the satisfactory within the human vocal take a look at in.

Finding your range isn't always very hard surely; you could start by means of manner of the usage of listening to the manner you speak. Does your voice tremble at the same time as you communicate? Do you have got a sweet, squeaky voice? Do you have got a mid-variety or easy voice? Take a microphone or voice recording software program and report yourself speakme. It can also appear silly in case you haven't completed this earlier than, and it's going to likely be clearly be brilliant in case you're listening to yourself talk via a third-party for the number one time. Your voice will sound oddly surprising because of the reality what you pay attention on your head at the same time as you talk isn't always a real example of what others without a doubt pay attention; because of the truth whilst we speak, sound doesn't only come from our vocal cords.

The manner we sound is carefully tormented by our sinuses, nasal hole space, and our bones as properly. Our sinuses and nasal hollow space have masses of vicinity wherein sound waves leap around earlier than they adventure to the recipient's ear. However, it's now not that the sound produced due to our sinuses and bone form alters the sound that escapes our our bodies that an awful lot. It doesn't. Rather, whilst we talk, we're paying attention to the vibrations taking place in our bones, in our nasal hollow area, and in our sinuses. This is why our voices sound so unique whilst we pay attention to a recording, and it's additionally why you may't without a doubt trust what you pay attention on a regular basis to decide your creating a tune voice. Chances are your real voice has less growth and bass, so preserve this in mind whilst looking for your variety.

After recording and listening on your voice range, allow's have a look at the pitch and the timbre. Pitch is how immoderate or low a valid is, at the same time as timbre is the uniqueness or character of the sound. To similarly recognize the concept of pitch and timbre, be aware that hardly ever any two singers sound exactly alike. For instance, Rihanna doesn't sound like Beyonce; Andrea Bocelli's sound is distinct from Luciano Pavarotti; and Whitney Houston doesn't sound like Mariah Carey. We all have a few element that makes the tone of our voices super. Your range can heavily rely upon this. You may have a immoderate sounding voice, however your timbre may additionally moreover moreover display that you can be more of an alto than a soprano. It's all approximately listening and reading your very very own one-of-a-kind characteristics.

Now that we've an concept how our voices sound at the same time as we communicate, it's time to pay attention to how we sound when we sing. This can be complicated in case you're doing this for the primary time. You may additionally need to make use of an tool, so enjoy loose to ask a guitarist or pianist pal of yours to help. You might also moreover use a essential song, like "Mary Had a Little Lamb." Almost in reality every body can sing a track like that, although it doesn't sound too correct. Record yourself and take note of the playback. Did you will be predisposed to go lower inside the track? Or were you greater cushty with the better notes? Listen to all of that when identifying your variety.

To make a extra accurate assessment, but, you'll need the help of a musical tool like a guitar or a piano. Ask a chum to play a "middle C" be aware, it sincerely is the C-be aware inside the path of the center of the piano, moreover called "C4" (see the diagram beneath). Try to duplicate the precise sound that you concentrate. This can also additionally help in schooling your ear. Aim to sing as close to as viable to the word that you concentrate. The purpose of this contemporary workout is not to be spot on, but to look how low or how excessive you can bypass. After middle C, flow into down the dimensions. If you may circulate below C3 (3 octaves lower), then maximum probably you're a bass. If you prevent spherical C3, and also you're able to float up above middle C all the way to E4, then you definately in reality are more likely a tenor. If you're able to cross in addition beyond E4 to an octave above that, you then definately are most probable an alto. If you're able to flow above that, then you definately virtually're a soprano.

All the ones sorts may be divided even similarly into subtypes. The one among a kind kinds of basses are in particular basso profundo (contrabass), bass, and baritone. They depend intently at the pitch of your vocal join up. Contrabasses are able to visit G1 and likely even lower – they may be able to obtain the lowest ends of the human sign in. There are tenors and there are countertenors. Countertenors have the best variety for the male vocal test in and might every now and then pass as excessive as a soprano in sturdy and smooth falsetto. Altos are divided into contralto and alto. Contraltos have the bottom variety for the female vocal sign up and may skip as little as a tenor or sometimes as low as a baritone. On the possibility hand, altos are capable of hit the lowest of the soprano variety. Sopranos, however, are divided into mezzo-soprano, soprano, and sopranino. Mezzo-sopranos have the bottom of the soprano variety and can flow into as an lousy lot as spherical G5, sopranos can sing as an awful lot as a C6, on the same time as sopraninos can go beyond that. Singing on the top notch and lowest prevent of the musical scale takes potential and innate abilties — and it is very unusual to find each.

Don't fear about figuring out your subtype right now. Once you've got found your primary range, it's time to get to paintings.

Chapter 14: Intro to Musical Scales

A musical scale is a succession of musical notes to be able to growth or decreases by way of manner of pitch. The "Do-Re-Mi-Fa-So-La-Ti-Do" all of us determined out in kindergarten or on Sesame Street or The Sound of Music is truly a musical scale. Try creating a tune it for your head. This scale mimics the most scale. We acquired't flow into an entire lot element approximately what makes it a prime scale, however it's miles vital to comprehend that track is comprised of these scales. "Do-Re-Mi" can be recited in a number of extraordinary keys. Think of a key because the notice you start on within the scale, so if you start at the center C word of the keyboard, then you are creating a music a scale in the key of C.

Ask a pal who has a piano that will help you with training the way to sing a scale. Learning a way to sing a scale is an essential important of tune and creating a track. Professionals exercising scales all the time, not only with their voice, however with devices as properly. Reciting scales facilitates you warmness up your voice in advance than a overall performance and trains your ears. This is specifically critical if you don't forget your self a tone-deaf man or woman. As stated in advance than, "Do-Re-Mi" is a superb scale, and it usually consists of seven unique notes. Once you get greater superior, you may observe more about special scales collectively with the minor scale. Major scales seem satisfied and fun, while minor scales sound mysterious and unhappy. Many of our modern-day-day R&B and dad songs are within the minor scale. You will consequences pay attention the difference if you ask your pianist pal to play a first-rate scale and minor scale.

Before you begin working towards your first scale, tell your associate on the piano or guitar to play the C number one scale numerous instances so you can concentrate it for your head. Listening to it again and again will make sure which you get it right. By this time, you have to already understand your variety, so ensure that you start on the proper C or you can run the hazard of going too high or too low. If you are a tenor or bass, a secure wager is to start on C3, while altos or sopranos are counseled to begin on C4 or middle C. Once you've got got listened to the size some times and might pay interest it really on your head, it's time to attempt making a song it.

Listen to the primary observe being executed. Don't skip at once to the following be conscious till you've got have been given the number one be conscious down pat. Proceed till you have had been given reached the very wonderful test, which need to be C once more. Congratulations, you have got certainly sung your first musical scale!

When creating a tune your scales, be careful not to transport too fast that lets in you to keep away from doing them improperly or singing the notes incorrectly. It is better to sing one be aware ten instances and get it proper, in choice to to sing the whole scale incorrectly ten instances. You need to teach your ear, and you may't try this in case you aren't listening and repeating the right be conscious properly. As such, repetition is crucial: If you have were given a trouble hitting the primary notes of the dimensions, don't go with the flow on until you're capable of hit it efficiently. Yes, it could get vintage virtually speedy, but once more, it's higher to do it proper than do it incorrect. If you're suffering, ask your buddy to play the scale again and again all all over again and try sincerely listening at the side of out making a song. After being attentive to it several more instances, then try growing a tune all of it another time.

After a few days or maybe weeks, you ought which will sing "Do-Re-Mi" with out using a keyboard in both ascending and descending order. Sing alongside in particular keys (starting with A in desire to C, for example), and you can alternative and sing "La-La-La" or a few element else in place of making a track "Do-Re-Mi",

Chapter 15: Learning Breath Control

Professional singers are often able to sing scales that span severa octaves. Some of them can even do this with one breath, regardless of the truth that creating a track the smooth scale is difficult enough in a unmarried breath. Singers discover ways to do this through breathing strategies to ply their exchange. If they don't, then they danger sounding awkward constantly taking quick brief breaths among terms and terms. Breathing in itself isn't hard; all of us recognise the way to respire. When it involves growing a track, however, it's far all about manipulate, and now not every body non-public that abilities. While you don't in reality should suppose even as you are respiratory truly; growing a tune, rather, calls for which you tell your thoughts while it's appropriate to inhale and exhale. This is why breath training can be very critical.

In the phrases of Robert C. White:

"In the Beginning there was Breath, and Singing end up with Breath, and Breath modified into Singing, and Singing was Breath. And all creating a track changed into made thru the Breath, and without Breath come to be now not any Singing made that become made."

One common difficulty is seen on this albeit humorous passage: You can't have making a song with out breath. Singing is really exhaling at the same time as vibrating your vocal chords. It's feasible to respire without singing, however it's not possible to sing without breathing.

Posture:

First, your posture need to be taken into consideration. Posture dictates how an lousy lot vicinity might be available for air to fill in your lungs. If you aren't repute or sitting properly, you may now not be able to exercising respiratory well.

When sitting, ensure that your again is right away. Do no longer lean again within the chair and don't slouch each. It is excellent to take a seat within the middle of the chair whilst creating a tune. Place your toes flat at the ground collectively with your hands each resting on your lap or protecting the sheet track. If you are preserving sheet song, have it leveled along side your chin and no decrease than your chest. It should be within the the the front of you and a long manner enough away that you'll be able to study the notes and phrases. Having your song to your lap will avoid sufficient respiratory thinking about that your head is tilted down.

When you're standing, make certain which you stand up right now and that your ft are flat at the ground. Your chest need to be pushed out a chunk as properly, as if you are feeling pleased with yourself. If you are retaining sheet song, observe the identical recommendations as if you had been sitting. If you don't have sheet music, preserve your hands on your aspects. Do now not bypass your hands closer to your chest or everywhere in the the front or in the again of you.

Inhalations:

Without inhalation, it'd be now not feasible to exhale, right? The trick is to find the right massive form of times to inhale at the same time as singing. Sometimes inhalation wants to be quite quick, on the equal time as at awesome instances, singers have greater than enough time in a track to relaxation and take in air.

A top singer is aware about a way to absorb sufficient air to complete a passage. It is important to learn how to inhale enough air in a fragment of a 2d in an effort to sing a passage that lasts for severa seconds or longer. When breathing in, you need to get the air into your belly and not allow it rest on your chest otherwise you obtained't find the gap to sing at the identical time as needed. Of course, the air isn't in reality entering into your stomach, but it ought to experience that manner due to the reality your diaphragm, the muscle that controls the hollow space below your lungs, is transferring downward to make space for your lungs to extend. The extra you permit your diaphragm pass downward, the greater air you are able take in.

Now do that very slowly. Take a while and pause amongst inhaling and then exhaling. Practice taking 5-second inhalations, five-2nd breaks (keeping your breath), and 5-second exhalations. Then begin lowering the time for inhaling and growth the time for breaks or exhaling. Afterwards, begin reducing the quantity of time to your breaks and range the instances in which you do each. When you breathe, ensure that you are pushing out your belly, no longer your chest. Your chest want to truly be the final issue to stretch whilst inhaling. Your diaphragm can stretch a excellent deal farther than your chest can, permitting you're taking in more air.

Exhalations:

Now it's time to begin education exhalations. One properly exercise professional singers practice is pressured exhalations. This is done with the aid of trying to get all of the air out to your lungs through unconventional strategies. Perhaps you've visible humans rumble their lips as a developing a song exercise?

If you don't know what that is, it seems like a loud bike or aircraft, and you may do it via sticking your lips out like a duck, but softly without flexing. Then push air out via them. Rumbling your lips wonderful we may want to as little air to go through as viable, for this reason this permits in sustaining exhalation. Practicing this sustained exhalation exercise will, through the years, will let you sing the ones excessive notes and long terms. This is what a singer objectives to do at the same time as making a song: use as little air as possible to get the clearest examine out.

Another such exercising includes working toward with a feather or leaf even as status or lying flat on your again: Place the feather for your lips and blow as difficult as you may to attempt to get the feather as immoderate as viable for as long as viable. Be excessive exceptional to keep one surrender with your fingertips.

Chapter 16: Improving your Diction for Singing

Unless you're utilising wordless melodies, pronunciation may be very essential in creating a track. Some people located diction final on the listing of factors they need to exercise near growing a track because they agree with diction is most effective important for public speakers. However, if you are trying to deliver a message thru song, it will in all likelihood be out of place if your purpose market can't apprehend you. This is why diction is so important.

Listen to any music — pop, classical, jazz, u . S ., any fashion you fancy — and you can find out which you are capable of apprehend all of the phrases despite the fact that sung softly. However, sometimes at the same time as you concentrate to those artists performing the same tune stay, it's a top notch tale. It's very easy to wander away within the tune, however terms are just as essential in a track. To have the ability to talk via your music, you need to be understood always. And to do this, you need to exercise diction wearing activities.

For diction, you have to use the same bodily games that public audio tool do. Start with clean sports and exercising the most essential trouble in making a track phrases: forming vowels. People regularly communicate otherwise than they sing, so don't anticipate pronunciations to be the identical. Pronouncing your vowels well will ensure the message remains the identical.

Diphthongs are vowels sounds referred to in a single syllable, like in "lane" or "hour". In the case of diphthongs, whilst we communicate, we observe the rule of thumb "the number one one does the talking, the second one maintains on walking." However, while we sing, each vowels are often said. We every now and then remodel even easy vowels into diphthong to accommodate their corresponding notes. Take the vowel "i" as an instance. Say the vowel over and over on your head. What do you pay attention? You will maximum probably concentrate the combination of awesome vowels, "a(h)" and "e(e)." This is how we pronounce our vowels in track. Let's exercising how we'd shape our vowels at the identical time as creating a music a easy phrase. Let's sing, "I am in love with you." Don't mind the melody but; we'll sincerely attempt to awareness on how we sing this phrase. When you are making a music this phrase, it want to sound some aspect like this: "Aeeh am een louv weeth yuu."

When we sing phrases, we're essentially growing a song vowels enveloped with the resource of consonants. To visualize, permit's don't forget a written letter. When we get a letter, are we able to be aware of the envelope? No, but the envelope is critical in delivering a letter. It's the equal with consonants – we shouldn't placed emphasis on them, but they will be even though very vital. We shape our consonants with our lips, teeth, and tongue. When you sing and also you need to maintain a word, we make bigger the vowel, now not the consonant. "Been," at the same time as extended as an example, want to be sung as "beeeeeen" now not "beennnnnnn".

When you are walking toward your diction, address your tongue and the way you operate it. Allow it to move approximately as it desires. Recite as many tongue twisters as you can. Another manner to exercise your diction is through recording your self and listening once more to it. A higher detail to do is to play it to someone else. If they could't listen all the words that you are saying, then you definitely definately want to hold working towards. Finally, take note of tremendous orators. Sure, they aren't developing a music, however concentrate to how they shape their phrases. Some of them have a examine the identical suggestions that singers do.

Chapter 17: Adding Vibrato

Vibrato is the vibration you pay interest at the same time as a person is making a song, particularly while they may be creating a track longer notes. To a novice, this is probably the trickiest method to understand. However, if you have mastered it and might perform it effects, you are for your manner to turning into a extremely good singer. It is viable to do it badly, even though, that could break the go with the flow and sense of your tune. A lousy vibrato is a horrible element to pay interest, so training a way to do your vibrato well is critical.

First, open the all over again of your throat. Some human beings attempt to sing vibrato with a closed throat, however it doesn't work that way. If you don't clearly realize what taking off the decrease back of your throat need to enjoy like, strive yawning. Feel and apprehend the mechanisms which can be taking location to your throat and mouth to take in and launch all that air. Next, loosen up yourself definitely, such as your chest and belly. A lot of humans try to do vibrato with a anxious stomach, which ends up in a pressured vibrato that is apparent even to a infant. Ensure that your posture is proper and you are breathing well, using the recommendations from Chapter 3.

Now that your frame is ready, you're prepared to start working towards and making a song the proper manner. If you have been schooling with the aid of making a song from your throat, STOP! It has been implied in advance than in this guide but we'll say it more in fact right here: The air you operate to offer notes must commonly feel find it irresistible's coming out of your diaphragm. Now sing one observe — possibly begin with a "Laaa." Again, don't forget that it want to revel in like it's popping out of your lungs, now not out of your throat. Be positive the be aware is at a pleasant pitch and attempt once more. Keep doing it over and over, only then looking to upload the vibrato. It will come quite clearly to you, but don't be disillusioned if you could't sing a clean vibrato right away. Just a chunk vibrato is improvement. It's an tremendous reminder no longer to pressure it. Not fine does a pressured vibrato sound terrible, however you may additionally damage your self. A right vibrato is continuously natural and diffused.

Vibrato isn't for each tune or each degree no matter the reality that. Vibrato is definitely a rapid fluctuation in pitch, and in case you do too much, you may fall in pitch. Vibrato is right to help add emphasis on passages, particularly on longer ones. Hearing vibrato on brief and brief phrases and passages sounds bizarre and forced. The handiest commercial enterprise corporation that has been capable to tug this off is Alvin and the Chipmunks, and we honestly don't want to sound like a novelty act.

There are times in effective kinds of tune at the identical time as you could want to exert a more pressured sort of vibrato. The vibrato in those instances allows to intensify a be aware or a phrase. You will frequently pay attention this on the quit of display tunes, classical track, or jazz songs. However, in maximum times, vibrato need to commonly come really. Remember that subtlety is the mark of resourceful splendor in music.

To assist boom your vibrato certainly through the years, try diaphragm wearing sports. Your diaphragm controls how nicely your vibrato is, so it lets in to do breathing bodily video video games to agreement and lighten up your diaphragm. You also can do short respiration physical video games in quick succession to gain this. One extra issue: at the identical time as Whitney Houston is the crucial instance of a super singer, she did some thing that you want to no longer exercise doing — moving your jaw up and down in brief succession to imitate the vibrato sound. Don't do this. Producing vibrato through your jaws is the wrong manner of creating a music.

Chapter 18: Singing and Your Attitude

If you want to be a terrific singer — a great singer even — then you'll need something to keep you going: the proper thoughts-set. If you start with the wrong mind-set, then you definitely without a doubt honestly're no longer going to attain very an extended way — and your voice obtained't both. If you experience like you may't sing very well, don't smile and repeat, "Oh, I can't sing," whenever a person asks you to sing some issue. If you really want to be an exceptional singer, and you are within the technique of mastering, then your reaction need to be, "I'm now not notable yet, however in case you need, I can attempt a few component." Having that form of extraordinary attitude will maintain you in the right frame of mind to maintain learning and shifting in advance. Hence, the primary feature which you need to work on is yourself guarantee.

Confidence is the critical aspect to telling your mind which you're hungry to maintain improving, despite the fact which you could not get topics right away. Don't be overconfident or cocky of course, as with a purpose to save you you from absolutely undertaking your true functionality, that can break your opportunities of being an splendid singer. Behaving that way tells your thoughts which you have executed your top and also you recognize all of it already. So when you have that mind-set, you certainly prevent getting to know. Nobody, now not even experts who make a residing making a song, have to have that thoughts-set. We are all despite the fact that getting to know. Author Isaac Asimov, whose works were preponderant of modern-day technological knowledge-fiction, stated as it should be "We simplest in fact prevent learning as quick as we die."

Set immoderate yet practical expectancies for yourself. If you are a bass, don't tell your self that you will be Luciano Pavarotti in a twelve months. You may be able to boom your variety, however by the point you have executed so, you furthermore may need to observe the opposite techniques to have the functionality to drag off a complex piece like "Nessu Dorma" successfully. If you're an alto, don't set an expectation a good way to sing the ones excessive notes in Mariah Carey's vintage songs. There's not anything incorrect with meaning to boom your range, but each person's voice is certainly one of a kind and unique. Some voices might be able to do what others can't. With that said, it does assist to set mini-wants to your creating a track schooling. These mini-goals ought to encompass gaining knowledge of a scale or two, being able to exhale for added than 10 seconds with only 1-2 seconds of inhalation breath, or a few thing that you can gather in a quick amount of time. From there, keep on building your capabilities, and you will recognize that the ones mini-goals have converted themselves cumulatively into big achievements.

Chapter 19: Warm-up the Voice

We will begin this ebook with vocal and respiratory sports. Don't get overwhelmed with the resource of the use of the technical info of the records. If you enjoy love it's too much, bypass ahead. Come lower returned to the number onechapters after reading approximately the attitude and the sensory experience. Give yourself time to soak in all of the facts with a great mind-set.

The first issue you need to recognise about creating a tune is that your entire body is your device. Many people believe that developing a track is living on your throat and vocal cords on my own. Every a part of your frame performs an vital feature in your achievement as a singer. The body isn't a difficult and fast tool like a piano that really wishes an occasional tuning and test-up. It is constantly converting each day and singers must work thru how the body is feeling that day.

Stretching & Posture

Now that we've got found out that your whole body is your device, it is essential to begin your creating a track consultation with a warmth-up. Doing yoga could be an first rate begin. If that isn't an opportunity then start with stretches inside the lower once more, neck and shoulders.

First arise and put your feet shoulder width aside. Reach your palms above your head and stretch within the path of the ceiling. Focus on elongating the again and alternate the gain with each arm. Then flop your frame over and contact your ft. Move your ft a chunk in addition aside after which allow skip of all of the muscle organizations to your upper body. Just draw near like a rag doll and allow gravity take all the tension far from your neck, shoulders and reduce once more. After 10-20 seconds of striking, slowly begin to roll your body as plenty because the repute role. Slowly enjoy your spine stack and the remaining issue to roll up is your neck and head. Next, have your left ear move inside the course of your left shoulder and take your left hand and vicinity it on the possibility facet of your head clearly above your proper ear. Hold the stretch for a few thing time you experience is needed after which repeat this same stretch at the opportunity trouble. Slowly begin to roll your shoulders ahead to lower once more, and however to in advance. Shake out your arms and legs. Then continue with some other stretch that you're feeling may be beneficial on your frame that day.

Next we can focus on posture for making a song. Correct posture and alignment is one of the key factors in discovering your proper making a tune voice. Stand along side your feet shoulder width aside. Your chest need to be open and lifted. Lift your shoulders up for your ears, pull them returned an inch and back off over again. Think of a kitchen toaster. Your shoulders arise out of 1 toaster hole and that they circulate back and down into the opposite toaster hole. With your hand, find out your sternum bone. Your sternum is placed under your collarbone and in the middle of your chest. Your sternum bone must constantly be lifted. Imagine a string connected for your sternum bone and then lifting the string upward. Be aware of your again. Try now not to arch the once more if you want to open the chest. This motives anxiety in the decrease lower back and will make subjects tough for respiratory. Your head and neck need to continuously emulate the Aristocracy. Notice how the royals in England maintain themselves. The head is continually lifted, shoulders square, with an open chest. You can also use the string workout with the pinnacle as well. Imagine a string related to the center of your head and pull it upward. With all of this artwork at the alignment to your frame, make sure which you aren't shielding muscle groups and growing an uncomfortable quantity of hysteria. Some of those postural corrections could be uncomfortable at the beginning. As you switch out to be privy to your alignment weaknesses, you may be more privy to correcting yourself inside the route of the day. The open, noble posture will begin to experience herbal. Refer to the image for incorrect vs.

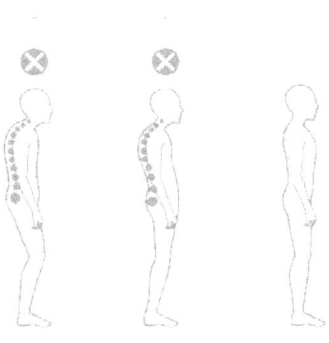

Accurate body alignment.

Breathing

Now we'll skip straight away to respiration carrying activities. Breathing for singing is particular than everyday respiratory for ordinary life. Breathing for making a song is going masses deeper inside the frame. When you inhale, the rib cage ought to extend and the stomach will boom out. Put one hand for your stomach and one to your rib cage. Now bear in mind your chosen scent. Imagine hot, chocolate brownies baking within the oven. While imagining that smell, take an extended, deep breath in. Feel the rib cage enlarge to the aspect and your belly increase out in the front. Now flow your hands onto your decrease lower back. Place them below your rib cage and proper above the pant line. Take that prolonged, deep, scrumptious inhalation again. You have to be capable of revel in that boom inside the yet again. If you are having a hard time, sit down in a chair. Then slightly lean over, region your hands on your back and attempt yet again. These respiratory sports activities need to not be rushed. Focus, and enjoy the deep breaths. Then take a second to find a mirror and move workout those deep breaths in the the front of it. You want to now not see the chest and shoulders upward push with deep respiratory. You have to sense increase beginning truely below your chest and underneath. Strive to usually have a downward gesture collectively along with your inhale. When a hint little one is asked to take a deep breath, what do they do? They suck in air very noisily and sing his own praises their chest as immoderate as they might. That is an upward gesture with the inhale. So permit's divide your frame intoparts. Just below the chest and beneath is the lower half of of your body. The chest and above is the better 1/2 of of of your frame. The top half is the quiet location and the decrease 1/2 is the active vicinity. Try deep respiration sooner or later of your day. You will enhance the muscles of the rib cage and it'll additionally beautify your highbrow fitness for the day!

Now I would love you to do a little stupid animal noises with those subsequent sporting sports. Think of the way a canine pants. They can pant all the time right? We are going to imitate canine pants in our rib cage. We will now not be able to drift as long as a canine can, but this workout builds the intercostal muscle businesses of the rib cage and strengthens them. So skip in advance, start sluggish ordinary pants. Now boost up the pants. Have fun with it and allow your tongue grasp out like a canine!

Let's keep with some monkey grunts! Is this getting bizarre but? I ought to point out that singers want to perform a little funny physical sports activities with their our bodies so that the whole body is worried in making a track. So we are going to carry out a touch low grunts like a monkey or a gorilla have to. Again, I experience like we should get into individual for this exercise! Bend your knees and get that center concerned. Do a few low 'hoo, hoo, hoo, hoo' noises. Think of a set of football gamers in a circle getting energized for a football recreation. Use your middle and rib cage muscle mass. These grunts are also correct for primal vocal sporting sports activities that I will deliver an cause of in some time.

Chapter 20: Warm-up the Articulators

Are you prepared to make some noise now? Let's begin with a few articulation warmness-ups. The articulators are your tongue, tooth, lips and mouth. Let's perform a little lip buzzes. Lip buzzes are the noises that little kids make while they're pretending to force a automobile. Take a deep inhale and permit the lips to return again collectively at the exhale. Start on the 5th be aware of a scale going on. So if we are within the key of C Major, start on the G above middle C, and descend G, F, E, D, C. I additionally want to offer the notes numbers. That makes it simpler for a few people. So in case you are not familiar with tune or the notes, then truely start on any word which you need within the center of your voice and descend five, four,3,2,1. For each new lip buzz, you may circulate to the study above the first-rate you started out inside the final exercising. Always begin with the very tremendous phrase first and then descend down from it. There is a cause for this and we are able to communicate it inside the subsequent financial spoil. So preserve doing the lip buzzes for five-8 mins. You need to regularly begin to encompass descending octaves or the 8th be privy to the size taking place 8,7,6,five,four,three,2,1. In this buzzing workout, experience free to explore the form of your voice a chunk.

Vocal Exercises

The important purpose for vocalizing (vocal exercising) is to educate our mind and the muscle corporations in our throat and body to undergo in thoughts the sensations of free uninhibited sound. So permit's find out vocal bodily sports that sell unfastened, launched sound. These wearing sports will assist perform your actual making a tune voice.

Primal Sound

We must begin this talk by using acknowledging Oren L. Brown. He emerge as a famous vocal pedagogue within the singing worldwide. He wrote the ebook "Discover Your Voice: How to Develop Healthy Voice Habits". This ebook had a large have an effect on in my vocal education all through my undergraduate years and I notably suggest it. I had the incredible privilege to attend and take part in numerous of his master training at my University. His attention on the use of primal sound in making a track changed me as a singer. He says:

"Primal sound…is the reflexive sound which produces emotional

expression. It is the sound you're making with out wondering on the identical time as, for instance, you're amused or startled or enraged." (Brown, 1996)

Incorporating vocal bodily video games that embody primal sounds may be huge in locating your proper singing voice. Let's discover moments at the same time as we use primal sounds in our everyday lifestyles. Can you bear in mind a conversation which you had with a person after they sincerely stored speaking and speaking all of the time? Then your responses within the verbal exchange just began out out to be brief little 'uh huh, uh huh' at the same time as nodding your head? Well the ones brief little 'uh huh' responses are primal sounds. These 'uh huh' sounds inspire a low launched function inside the throat and larynx. This is the right characteristic for developing a track. So allow's positioned those 'uh huh' sounds in a vocal exercise. Begin by way of the usage of slowly pronouncing 'uh huh, uh huh' in a low tone. Then have the closing 'uh' stay the low spoken sound, observed with the useful useful resource of creating a tune the final 'huh' at the descending five be conscious vocal workout. See display off A.

Exhibit A:

Speak 'uh huh, uh huh, uhhhhhhhh —- 'huh'

5 'hu

four u

3 u

2 u

1 uh'

This is to encourage that low primal launch of the throat (larynx) at the equal time as creating a track. Try to not experience a huge bounce/motion upwards to your throat whilst you begin to sing. Do this vocal exercising within the center range of your voice to start with. Think about times on your normal existence if you have felt this primal launch of sound. Crying? Sobbing? Laughing? These are all primal sounds which can be right to you and

inspire a low, free launch for your throat.

Descending Exercises

So why need to we usually start those vocal physical video video games with the pleasant be aware first after which maintain in a descending pattern? The first word which you sing has the fullest amount of air in your lungs and offers the nice air pressure to hold your vocal cords collectively. This strain decreases because of the truth the air leaves your lungs. If you start making a song on a decrease pitch after which ascend up five notes to the very splendid word, you could have the least amount of air for that highest be conscious. This will boom the opportunities of the singer having tension inside the throat and the sound will no longer be loose. So for the amateur singer all the manner as masses due to the fact the advanced, I advocate which you start your warmth-u.S.A.With descending vocal wearing activities. As you increase as a singer and characteristic a sturdy stability inside the body and throat, then it is probably appropriate to explore ascending vocal bodily video games. I've taught voice for over 20 years and creating a music for plenty longer than that. I though begin each making a song consultation with descending vocal wearing events.

The 'ring' to your tone

These next vocal bodily games are that will help you find the hoop for your resonance. Some name it the ping or the position of the sound. Let's start off thru doing a voiced 'th' sound. The voiced 'th' is the sound you are making in terms like 'that' or 'this'. We are going to do the voiced 'th' sound on the very pleasant word inside the 5 phrase word. So sing 'th' on examine five, then open it to the [i] vowel. You are creating a tune the very closed [i] vowel like within the phrase 'thee'. Then descend down the five notes at the [i] vowel. See show off B.

Exhibit B:

voiced 'th' ——- 'thee'——-

5 thee

4 ee

three ee

2 ee

1 ee

Strive to experience the presence of the resonance in the route of the exercise. Aim to feel the resonance within the masks of the face. Think of the masquerade masks worn at some point of the eyes, cheekbones and nostril. There are resonating cavities located inside the masks of the face and this is wherein you have to revel in the resonance. Don't be afraid if the resonance feels clearly exceptional, in advance or within the nostril. It's going to experience awesome than you're used to. It will revel in nosey, but now not nasal. We don't want to revel in the presence of the resonance inside the decrease returned of the mouth or throat. Resonating in those areas will no longer help you sing together with your right, unfastened sound. The satisfactory of the vocal resonance will sound protected and like you are trying to mimic a person else. Notice the subsequent image. I'm no longer going to go into superb detail approximately all of the anatomy pictured, but word the vicinity of the Nasal Cavity. Look at all of the resonating place available to you inside

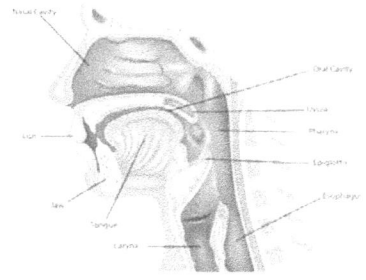

the masks of the face.

The next vocal workout that we will talk will help you collectively collectively together with your immoderate notes, your sign in transitions and an commonplace revel in of wherein every pitch to your voice need to resonate. You will sing on a 'thee' starting at the 8th tone of an 8 study scale. Think of the "Do-Re-Mi" song from the musical "Sound of Music". Do-Re-Mi-Fa-Sol-La-Ti-Do can be tones 1,2,three,four,5,6,7,8 in the ones physical games. You will descend in pitch beginning at the eighth (Do) to the 5th (Sol) to the third (Mi) and finishing on 1st (Do). You will right away open to the [i] vowel on 'thee'. See exhibit C.

Exhibit C:

8 thee

five ee

three ee

1 ee

Again, your goal is to have nosey resonance on each pitch. As you determine this vocal exercising and ascend to the higher test in of your voice, you'll want to take into account inner area. You also can have heard this earlier than at the same time as human beings say 'supply or enhance the easy palate'. That is growing the internal place that we want, but I sense like singers can misread the phrase 'elevate the smooth palate'. I misunderstood it for years. I would possibly over stretch the gentle palate. Doing this creates an excessive amount of area and the back of the throat is uncomfortable. It results in resonance falling manner once more into my throat. Then I ought to get remarks that I wanted extra 'ring' in my resonance and to carry it ahead. I may also proceed to take a look at the schooling and the stop stop result modified into a depressed tongue, excessive anxiety in my throat and a pushed/pressed sound.

Chapter 21: Think pitch

Something else that is very vital with this precise vocal exercising is the method. So many people think that we want to help excessive notes by the use of accomplishing or pushing for them. We in no manner want to visualise that the immoderate notes are way up inside the sky above us and that we need to climb up to fulfill them. This will frequently create anxiety in the throat. Instead, count on the pitch to your thoughts, create the about to sneeze area and recollect falling into the pitch from above. The sensation of descending proper right into a examine from above is a lot more thrilling than accomplishing and pushing for it with the throat. One of my favored mind from Oren Brown's e-book is:

"Our voice will display us what it may do for us, rather than our

pushing to make it do anything. The key

terms right proper right here are

count on, allow, and do not forget."
(Brown, 1996)

Sing through this vocal exercising and test
the bounds of your upper variety. The
concept approach and technique need to
be broken down into severa pieces at the
beginning. As you still workout, the
portions of the puzzle may be extra
established in your muscle reminiscence
and herbal for you. See show off D for the
idea way inside the 8, five, three, 1, 'thee'
exercising.

Exhibit D:

Deep inhale———- THINK primal 'huh' on your throat

Have the 'about to sneeze' notion for the slight palate improve

THINK fall into pitch from above

FALL into the resonating vicinity inside the mask of the face

Then Sing!

Sing on the gesture of the inhale

In monetary destroy one, we touched the difficulty of breathing for creating a tune. We need to have deep, low breaths and revel in the boom on all components of the ribcage. Here is the BIG element. After you inhale deeply, what do you do subsequent? Some humans hobby on having a good belly wall and barely pushing the breath. Let's speak a respiration technique this is more snug.

When you're taking in a breath, you need the inhale to be silent. When you gasp with the inhale, it creates a few tension for your throat and might make the respiratory method disturbing. So generally strive for a silent, non-gaspy inhale. My voice instructor continuously used to inform me to 'breathe through my ears'. Well that's not feasible of route, but simply attempt doing it and be conscious what occurs! The surrender quit result is a silent, deep inhale.

Now for the best aspect! When you launch the air to sing, you want to try and keep the gesture of the inhale in the body or hold to sing at the gesture of the inhale. The silent, downward inhale gesture creates intensity and a feel of ease to your throat. It moreover continues the rib cage energized for the air go with the flow. Now you want to keep rethinking the inhale gesture over and over all once more. This way the rib cage remains open and energized in your vocal phraseology. These are the mind to must your breath so you can slow the ascent of the diaphragm. The diaphragm is an up-aspect down, bowl standard, muscular membrane that is associated with the lowest of the rib cage. When singers inhale deeply, the diaphragm flattens out and pushes all of the guts of your belly out of the way. When you exhale, the diaphragm returns to its resting bowl-regular feature. The reason in singing is to gradual the ascent of the diaphragm on the same time as exhaling and to preserve the intensity in the breath.

www.ingramcontent.com/pod-product-compliance
Lightning Source LLC
Chambersburg PA
CBHW071335120626
46546CB00002B/567